PRAISE FOR *MINIMALIST MOMS*

"Diane is a wealth of easy tips and hacks as well as mindset shifts that can help you rehaul your physical and mental clutter!"

—Felica Allen, host of *Find the Magic* podcast

"Diane Boden takes a sledgehammer to the clutter in your life, giving you the freedom to focus on family, love, and all that's important."

—Ali Wenzke, author of *The Art of Happy Moving*

"*Minimalist Moms* is an elegant guide for those who are finding motherhood overwhelming. She walks you through the mindset shifts and practical steps needed to curate what truly matters so that you can regain the time and energy to be present in your life."

—Meg Nordmann, author of *Have Yourself a Minimalist Christmas*

"*Minimalist Moms* is that book that needed to be written. Diane gives such practical, realistic advice that I truly believe every mother needs to read this book. /

I am constantly telling clients that they need to declutter the contents of their home. Diane really captures the physical process of decluttering and the emotional side of things and gives people a good picture of the reason for minimalism that can be done specifically for you, in your home. The word minimalism can be a scary thing for people but Diane really shows just how realistic the concept can and should be in your home."

—Rachel Rosenthal, professional organizer

"If you want to address the physical and mental clutter that comes with the day-to-day experience of motherhood, this book is for you. An inspiring read that will help you scale back and enjoy motherhood to its fullest."

—Robyn Conley Downs, author *The Feel Good Effect* and podcast host

"*Minimalist Moms* is an invaluable resource in this era of 'too much.' Diane Boden cuts through the overwhelm and gives us a clear and simple path out of the clutter to a life filled with more peace and ease. With clear writing and an honest, relatable voice, this book is exactly what moms need!"

—Hunter Clarke Fields, author of *Raising Good Humans*

"Diane has beautifully curated this book to train, encourage and simplify your life when it comes to consuming less. *Minimalist Moms* is a book you need to read now, and continually refer back to for the rest of your life. Has minimalism ever intimidated you? Made you feel anxious? Then you need this book. It is gracious and relatable on all levels. Five stars!"

—Sarah Therese, YouTube influencer

"Diane Boden transforms minimalist parenting from a pipe dream to a tangible lifestyle for readers seeking lives of intention. And because Boden aptly explains the 'why' behind minimalism, mothers will find themselves enthusiastic about enacting her countless simplification strategies."

—Stephanie Marie Seferian, author of
    Sustainable Minimalism

"Simplicity always sounds and looks so simple, but the journey there often requires laying a foundation first. Diane outlines the steps needed to prepare for a more simplistic approach to parenting, while also digging deeper with personal discussion questions throughout the book."

—Eda Schottenstein, author of *Sarah Dreamer*

minimalist moms

minimalist moms

LIVING AND PARENTING WITH SIMPLICITY

diane boden

CORAL GABLES

Published by Mango Publishing Group, a division of Mango Media Inc.

Cover, Layout & Design: Morgane Leoni
Cover Photo: © JP_3D / Adobe Stock
Photos: © Diane Boden / Adobe Stock

For permission requests, please contact the publisher at:

Mango Publishing Group
2850 S Douglas Road, 2nd Floor
Coral Gables, FL 33134 USA
info@mango.bz

For special orders, quantity sales, course adoptions and corporate sales, please email the publisher at sales@mango.bz. For trade and wholesale sales, please contact Ingram Publisher Services at: customer.service@ingramcontent.com or +1.800.509.4887.

Minimalist Moms: Living and Parenting with Simplicity

Library of Congress Cataloging-in-Publication number: 2021930098
ISBN: (p) 978-1-64250-509-2, (e) 978-1-64250-510-8
BISAC category code FAM032000—FAMILY & RELATIONSHIPS / Parenting / Motherhood

Printed in the United States of America

This book is dedicated
to my children.

Without whom I'd have a much
cleaner home but fewer anecdotes
for a book on motherhood.

CONTENTS

HOW TO USE THIS BOOK

My original vision for *Minimalist Moms* was to create a
community of mothers that encouraged one another to
pursue a life with less—less clutter, less stress, less hurry.
The contents and structure of this book were intentionally
designed to help you achieve success with minimalism in your
home, mind, and schedule. To achieve this in a realistic way,
I've organized things into a few **areas of focus**. At the end of
each area of focus, I challenge you to pursue the theme on
your own. It doesn't matter if that area of focus takes you one
week or six months. Continue to pursue the thought until you
feel you've mastered it, then come back and choose another.

As I say throughout this book, slow steps add up to real
change. You don't have to declutter every area of your home
(and mind) before seeing changes. Stick with it.

For those of you looking to slowly declutter your life, my
suggestions to you would be:

1. After you read through the beginning of the book, step
    away for a day or so. Once you've read my story about
    the benefits of minimalist motherhood and learn why
    we become minimalists, really digest the information
    and decide whether or not minimalism is something
    you actually see yourself implementing. It's a lifestyle

change. Therefore, it's important to first take an assessment of your home with fresh eyes.

2. Cast your vision for minimalism onto your family. In what areas do you desire the most change? Your home? Your children's activities? Your calendar? Your work-life balance? Toys? Write it down.

3. Figure out what would be the biggest game changers for you and get to work!

4. Choose one area of focus and challenge yourself each month (or week)—whatever feels achievable right now.

5. After your initial decluttering/simplification of your home and schedule, continually pursue a life without excess. Come back to the areas of focus as needed.

This book is complemented by the *Minimalist Moms Podcast* with additional information and resources from guests in various areas of minimalist living. For more information, subscribe to the podcast or listen to the episode archive at www.minimalistmomspodcast.com.

Lastly, Minimalist Moms are a community. I want you to find encouragement from women pursuing this lifestyle all around the world. It doesn't look the same for every one of us, but you may find similarities in another mom's story. Share or mention the book on social media with the hashtag #minimalistmoms all over the web.

MY MINIMALIST STORY

Minimalism. What was once a term among a niche of green-minded people is now a mainstream idea. Do a quick search and you'll find hundreds of books on simplifying, decluttering, or the promise of "life-changing magic." While I could write a step-by-step guide to decluttering your home, many before me have already done so (and quite well, I might add).

What I desired to provide when I began this book was more of a quick, daily reminder of the impact of minimalism. We moms are busy, so this is a book of inspirational guidance that you can dwell on daily. Minimalism is more of a way of life than a

place one arrives at, after all. We need little reminders to keep that in perspective and focus on what's important to us.

I was quite the opposite of a minimalist in my late teens and early twenties. I was someone that needed a new outfit (or at least a new top) each time I attended church. I hated wearing the same combination of clothing more than once every couple of months. I wanted the newest, shiniest things, and every time I'd set foot into the mall or a Target (where I did most of my shopping at the time), I felt an almost compulsive pull toward the display laid before me. I was living paycheck to paycheck due to my spending habits. But wait—I'm getting ahead of myself. Let me take you back to the first time I realized I could buy without really thinking about the repercussions.

My desire to consume started long before I became an adult, but I remember the day when it was no longer up to my parents to control my spending. I held the power. It began on my eighteenth birthday. I headed to our local mall to get a new outfit for my celebratory dinner. As I roamed around Macy's with an armful of clothing, a sales associate stopped and asked if she could get a fitting room started for me.

As we talked, I casually mentioned that it was my eighteenth birthday and she responded by asking if I had any interest in opening up a credit card. Who, me? At the time, I was just looking forward to college. I hadn't thought about the other opportunities that this milestone birthday would bring. But people were actually interested in loaning me money? Sign me up. After trying on a couple of dresses and tops, I headed to the checkout area where I was met again by the sales associate. As she rang up my items, I showed her my driver's license and delivered my social security number, and was offered a two hundred dollar credit limit. (Looking back, I laugh at how naive I was to be thrilled by access to two hundred dollars, but at the time, it was like I'd hit the lotto.)

My original plan was to only purchase one top or dress for my birthday dinner, but I could now purchase all of the items I had taken into the dressing room. Charge it! A few weeks later, I received my two hundred-dollar Macy's bill with a little box at the top that said my minimum payment was only about twelve dollars. I was in disbelief. I walked out of the store with a bag full of new clothes and only had to pay twelve dollars for them that month.

You can obviously see the failed thought process of my plan. If I were to just pay the minimum payment, I'd only be whittling away at interest charges—something I didn't realize at the time of opening the credit card. I do think there is a problem with the lack of real-life economics education in schools, but that's an argument for another day. In my naive teenage mind, I could just pay small amounts until I was back to zero, then charge the card right back up again. This behavior continued on for the next couple of years until I was twenty years old and buried under six thousand dollars' worth of credit card debt.

The more I filled up my closet, the happier I became (or so I thought).

As you might have experienced, one of the problems with compulsive spending is that the high of the purchase is fleeting. It's not long until you find yourself at the store, on the hunt for the next item to fill your space. After a series of conversations, extra hours of work, and help from my parents, I was fortunate enough to be released from my debts. I recognize that this privilege isn't available to everyone. I did have help—I won't pretend that I did it on my own. That said, it was around this point that I realized I could no longer continue living paycheck to paycheck. I wasn't exactly sure how I'd break free of the hold that spending had over me. I knew I wanted to overcome the pull, but...how would I actually get there?

Flash forward three years later to a moment that transformed my life. Gone were the days of living above my means. I was married and had someone else helping me navigate finances and budgeting. I was still in college and my husband had just begun his second year of teaching, so we weren't exactly raking in the dough, but we were staying afloat well enough. One chilly autumn afternoon, my husband and I found ourselves on the hunt for something in my parents' basement. As we were down there, my husband said something to me that I'll never forget: "Think of how many hours they [my parents] have spent working to pay for these things that are now in boxes." I stood there and looked at everything in storage. Whoa. I'd never realized it before. My parents' hard-earned working hours were here, but at the same time, they weren't really—they were hidden away in boxes. All of that clutter used to be money. In the moments that followed, I found myself pondering: *Does anyone ever come down here and go through these things? Do my parents even know what they have here? If so, why are they storing these many things?* My husband's strong statement really made me rethink my priorities on where I wanted to direct my time, energy, and money moving forward.

Before I go on with the story, I do want to be sure to say this: it's okay to have things in boxes that were once well-loved. They weren't wasted work hours if they once brought your family joy. Those moments are priceless. However, I do think we need to consider *why* we keep things, and be intentional about what we're consuming and bringing into our homes. I tell you this story simply because it was a pivotal moment for me. When it comes to the things we keep, it's very personal. Some people have more of a sentimental pull to their possessions, some people don't know where to begin, and some people simply don't have the time. Others feel comforted by the sheer number of possessions they own. I don't want anyone to read this and think I'm throwing my parents under the bus for their way of life; the moment was merely something that got the ball rolling toward a different kind of life for *me*. I will forever be grateful for the childhood my parents gave me. Yes, it involved toys, but I think what's most important is that it involved *them*.

Back to the basement…It was truly that interaction that set my attention on the pursuit of experiences over possessions. Looking back, it seems unimaginable that a few words could change the nature of who I had been, but it's the truth. Up to that point, I hadn't realized that my consumerism led to not just debt, but stress and anxiety. It was dissatisfying. I had a closet crammed full of clothes, but I constantly found myself with "nothing to wear." In the days before meeting my husband, I lived paycheck to paycheck, the stress of which was a constant force (despite my not recognizing it at the time). I'm grateful to have married a man with discernment regarding finances. But even though that aided in my

decisions to stop spending as much, I was still left discontented. What really changed me was minimalism.

While my journey to minimalism didn't happen overnight, I slowly began implementing changes that aligned unconsciously with minimalist principles. I gradually began staying out of stores. I told myself to limit trips to the mall, to stop buying things I *wanted* rather than *needed.* I took inventory of what I owned and purged what was no longer useful or necessary to our household. The sense of freedom was almost instantaneous. I couldn't believe it. I never would have expected that possessions could put such weight on my life, but once I began to rid myself of these items, there was no turning back.

My husband and I began to work on a budget and set financial goals. This allowed us to home in on what was important to us and where we wanted to spend our money and attention. Something as simple as choosing either drinks or dinner on a date night (not both) allowed us some wiggle room. We chose not to purchase cable. We didn't want to be tied to the television—and honestly, our computers were distracting enough! We truly did become *mindful* of our purchases and how exactly we wanted to spend our money.

As a thirty-something woman now, I am remarkably different. Of course, I attribute some of this to age and experience, but I mostly owe it to my pursuit of minimalism. I want to be completely transparent with you, reader. Minimalism didn't completely change my life overnight. At the time of this writing, I've been at it for ten years and there are still areas of my life that need a bit of purging. I'm better at decluttering my home than my schedule. I believe in quality over quantity, but I still purchase paper plates from time to time. Minimalism has seeped into all areas of my life, but the transformation process for each area takes time.

We the minimalist mom community have discovered that the pursuit of things always leaves us feeling discontent and wanting more. When we take the time to recognize the value of the possessions we already own, we're left in a state of gratitude instead of longing.

GAME CHANGERS

At this point, I want to share some of the game changers that really affected how my husband and I were experiencing life. Note: We didn't necessarily accomplish these in a particular order, they happened organically as we began to live with more intention. Put together your unique action plan. Notice what little steps you need to take and *just begin*.

First and foremost: **stay out of stores**. I cannot repeat this tip enough. Few things make me as discontent as walking through a department store and feeling the compulsion to buy something I know is not a necessity. Of course, there will be instances when you'll need to go shopping, but if you find that you're regularly spending your downtime perusing online sales, it's time to re-evaluate. This does take some time, but after a while you'll be able to go to the store with your purchase in mind and not be swayed by the shiny, new things. (Please remember, marketers are making the things "shiny" to entice you on purpose. It's their job to get you hooked! Remain strong and do not fall for constant, ever-shifting trends.)

I'm also a big believer in **quality over quantity**. There's a sense of accomplishment when you save up for something nice that you don't have to regularly replace. I can't tell you how glad I am to own Birkenstock sandals that have lasted me three years, as opposed to the Old Navy flip-flops I'd have to replace a couple of times per summer. This is just one example, but there are plenty of others I could name: couches, handbags, appliances (I love my Vitamix!). What "quality" item(s) could you save up for to replace the mediocre item(s) you already own?

Another notable change in our lifestyle was **setting boundaries** with family members when it came to gift-giving. I have more to say about this in a later section (specifically when we discuss holiday minimalism), but I wanted to note

its importance now. It can be tough to express your lifestyle changes to family members, but I've found it helpful for people to understand where we're coming from when we say we're "minimalists."

One request we made to our family was to prioritize experiential gifts over things. Instead of bombarding my children with gifts at their birthdays, a lot of my relatives choose to instead take them out to lunch, a movie, the trampoline park, or mini golfing. It's not that my children don't receive gifts—they do. But by putting the experiential gift idea out there, I combat some of that excess, and maybe even get an afternoon to myself while the "gift" is taking place!

I'll conclude my minimalism story with a reminder: you'll never arrive at a place without *any* clutter. Others may disagree with

me, but in my experience as a mother of three, decluttering is something that is done consistently with intention. Children (especially more than one) will regularly bring in new "treasures" and toys. Move forward with confidence as you navigate what to save, what to photograph, and what to responsibly get rid of.

If you aren't diligent, clutter always has the capability of overwhelming your home. Even after ten years of this pursuit, I regularly have to go back through gifts my children have received, mail, clothing we no longer need, and dried out craft supplies, among a litany of other things. In different seasons, I've allowed the mail to multiply on the countertop, and artwork to linger unsorted.

I'm not the perfect minimalist, but of course, none of us are. The whole idea around here is to "think more and live with less." My hope is to inspire you as you pursue a life of less physically, emotionally, mentally, and spiritually. What looks like less to you won't look the same to me. We're all at different places on this journey, and I look forward to you joining the Minimalist Moms community!

WHAT ADVICE WOULD YOU GIVE TO SOMEONE WHO IS INTERESTED IN PRACTICING MINIMALISM BUT DOESN'T KNOW *WHERE* OR *HOW* TO START?

Start in the bathroom! I know it sounds kind of bizarre—why would you curate this space when you're only in it to shower and, ahem, use the toilet? In reality, it's a great place to start because it's usually the smallest place in your home. Rid the space of old bottles, expired prescriptions, toiletries you never intend to use, towels that have seen better days, and any knickknacks taking up precious counter space. I've never gotten rid of something that I've looked back on and regretted. If you haven't used an item in three to six months, you're probably never going to use it, and if need be, it can be replaced down the road. It's my belief that when we begin the decluttering process by category (say, clothes), we'll stumble across sentimental items that we're not quite ready to part with. Bathrooms don't typically hold items of sentimental value, so begin in there and gain the momentum of minimalism in one space of your home.

MINIMALIST MOTHERHOOD

Did my practice of minimalism change when I became a mother? No! You may still be skeptical about minimalism's possible applications in motherhood. I don't blame you.

Maybe you can't stop thinking about your preschooler, who regularly brings home beads they found in the school play-yard (or is this just my child?).

Maybe you're imagining your five-year-old, with pockets full of rocks, sticks, and "treasures" that they unload onto the coffee table daily.

Perhaps you're reminded of your eight-year-old, who loves trading collections with their friends on the bus (Shopkins, Pokémon, Pogs—whatever the craze of the age may be).

Or maybe you're visualizing your teenager's overflowing closet. You're thinking that you may as well throw in the towel now—there's no helping that disaster zone.

I'll admit that examples such as these *are* tricky to navigate, but I think the hardest realization is this: we don't have total control over other human beings and the "excess" they bring into our homes. Sure, we can set boundaries, but is the process even worth it? I'm here to tell you it *is*.

You can absolutely live with less. Adding members to your family doesn't anchor you to a lifetime of clutter. You are the parent and you get to make the rules for the home. That's not to say there won't be occasional pushback, but the lessons you teach your children will influence them as they continue to build on life skills to prepare for adulthood.

In fact, the process of decluttering your home can help your children learn to cope in a society of excess. It empowers them to make decisions and set boundaries for the future. Our entire lives revolve around learning how to fit things into certain borders. Learning these foundational habits as soon as possible is to their benefit.

Know that as you begin demonstrating the practice of minimalism, children of all ages will notice. Once your kids start to understand, they will follow along. You probably won't have to work as hard to keep their possessions curated. A smaller, more manageable quantity of toys will allow for more engagement and less decision fatigue during playtime.

When it comes to my personal experience, I say it's never too early to share your family values with your children. My husband and I have personally expressed the joy of purchasing experiences over things. Of course, there will be times when we're inside a store (or are sent through a gift shop after exiting the manatee exhibit—thanks, zoo) and my child asks for a new toy. In these moments, I say to her, "Let's put that on your wish list!" We'll take a picture of the item with my phone or jot down the item in my notes app. This saves us a public tantrum and also gives us a gift idea for when a birthday or Christmas rolls around. It's also okay to simply say "no." As minimalist moms, we want to prepare our children for the real world, so "no" will be good for them to hear every once in a while—we want to set our children up for success!

INVOLVE YOUR CHILDREN IN THE PROCESS

When it comes to decluttering your children's possessions, you only have a handful of options:

1. You're *not* going to deal with it. It's too difficult, so you just allow them to keep what they have and stick to your own things. To summarize: you do nothing.

2. You're going to declutter while they're not paying attention. It's unfair for you to read this book or listen to the podcast and then immediately head to your children's rooms to get rid of "all the things." I don't know about you, but it doesn't seem right to declutter without them being involved. Can you imagine if someone took away something that really mattered to you? You may figure, "Oh, they won't notice this is missing," but that's not the best way to build trust and communication. Not to mention, the sneakiness usually backfires (especially with older children) and might create an instinctive need in them to want to hoard.

3. You're going to involve them in the process. My decluttering process has included a mixture of options two and three. It's important to regularly engage in dialogue with your children so they can learn the discipline themselves. Explain to them why you've decided to declutter your home and purge the things you no longer deem essential. If you don't like the idea of making those decisions for them (especially with older children), get them involved!

|||

Your children need to learn the responsibility of keeping and caring for their own things. I don't think it's realistic to think your kids will be overly enthusiastic about purging their toys, but they can help! They may surprise you with their ability to understand and help the process move along.

A good starting point is storage containers, as they provide visual boundaries. You can discuss what each container will hold, but you'll ultimately have the final say on how many you'll store in your home. For the process itself, set a timer for fifteen minutes and see how much you can tidy and organize in that time. Don't overwhelm your children with more than this—keep the process feasible. If toys aren't an issue, drawers and closets are other spaces to declutter and organize. Let them help!

As they grow, continue to include them in the conversation. Explain the process in a mature way—they'll understand more than you think! It can be something as simple as stating, "We can keep five of these items. Which ones are really special to you and which ones do you want to donate?" or "When you're done using [fill in the blank], who do you think it could go to?" Knowing who they're gifting the items to can be really helpful. It puts a face to the donation, as opposed to dropping it at a donation center, never knowing who (if anyone) will own the item. They can imagine who is enjoying it—a friend, cousin, or neighbor. Something I've found helpful with my children is instilling the concept of having things for a time, but not forever. Our children will be more empathetic and giving as they grow if we help them create this foundation.

All in all, keep in mind the importance of your relationship. With children, it's inevitable that things will come into the house. You don't want to feel like you're depriving them because that can ultimately backfire. Keep your relationship at the forefront of your mind as you navigate this. It's not worth yelling, or being harsh or demanding. If they aren't ready, don't push too hard. Continue to live by example and regularly prompt the idea of decluttering.

> "It's very hard because everything you like is in your room, but it's special to other kids and every kid needs it. They will be really happy and that makes me really happy, too."
> —Charlotte Boden, five years old

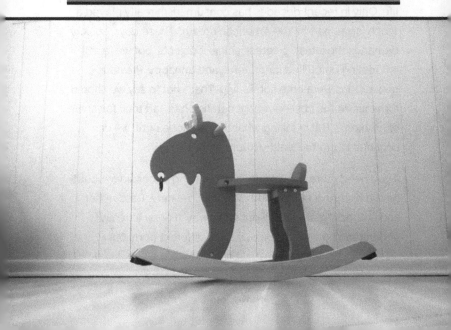

MINIMALIST MOTHERHOOD AND A CONNECTION TO THE PAST

Throughout my motherhood experience, I've always appreciated insight from others that have gone before me. Let's take that idea a bit further. We can glean a lot of wisdom from different cultures, or even just by taking a look at the way that people lived fifty to sixty years ago. Their desire to consume looked very different. I'm sure a lot of you have heard this 1900s wartime motto: "Use it up, wear it out, make it do, or do without." It was during this time in history when Americans were called upon to be frugal and practice intentionality when purchasing, because instant gratification and resources were scarce. I admire this mindset. Not only does it save money, but it's environmentally-friendly and benefits all aspects of life. Only in recent decades has consumerism really played a much larger part in "the American dream." These days, society demands the latest, greatest, shiniest objects, but we're still left feeling unfulfilled, ungrateful, and unhappy. Previous generations were onto something. That's not to say we should romanticize the past—every generation has had their fair share of problems. But in taking what they've done right, we can continue to craft a healthy future for ourselves.

If you need more convincing, another thing to consider would be the history of humankind. Stay with me here. Researcher and author William Rathje put it this way, "For us to really understand how we are similar to, or different from, our ancestors, we must be able to look at ourselves in ways which are comparable to the way we look at past societies." Minimalism wasn't trendy in the past, nor was the general idea of living with less. It was merely good housekeeping without emphasis on consumerism. Most people lived within their means and without excess. Nowadays, we live in the most materially rich society in global history, with light-years more possessions per average family than any preceding society. As the book *Life at Home in the Twenty-First Century* says, "While elites and royalty of earlier eras often lived amid great affluence at stunningly furnished palaces—Versailles comes to mind—the average European household of this time was sparsely appointed."

Think all the way back to nomadic cultures. There's no way to live with abundance when you're on the move from location to location. At that point in human history, people didn't have what they couldn't make or grow—there was a limit to how much a person could accrue. I get that this is a bit of a stretch for the modern mind, but I wanted to take you to this point to make you see that "needing" everything we can afford is truly a modern mindset.

THE BENEFITS OF MINIMALIST MOTHERHOOD...

IN FRIENDSHIPS

Friendships are a crucial part of the motherhood experience. Not only do fellow mom friends provide a fun excuse to schedule playdates, but they, too, are navigating the challenges and overwhelming emotions of raising children.

You may wonder why I'm choosing to focus on friendships right now—after all, this is a book on minimalism. I want to present a concept to you that might be slightly controversial, but I can't leave it out when talking about the game changers that ultimately benefited my minimalist approach to

motherhood. This particular shift has to do with the depth and number of relationships in my life.

A couple of years after my daughter was born, I was finding it difficult to maintain all the various friendships in my life. I had friends from college, previous churches I'd attended, and small groups, as well as individuals I just met along the way. I got to a place where I knew it was impossible to maintain a healthy quality in all of these relationships. At the time, I was almost a mother of two and I knew I could no longer pour myself into all of these women. Something had to give.

I sat down with a pen and paper. On one side, I wrote out all of the women I was currently interacting with. On the other, I wrote out "Tier One," "Tier Two," and "Tier Three." I then rewrote the names under the tiers. Based on this system I constructed, the individuals in "Tier One" were women I'd want to see weekly (or at the very least, bi-weekly), the women in "Tier Two" were friends I'd want to see (at minimum) once a quarter, and in "Tier Three" were the women I still loved and cared for, but no longer had time to pursue.

For me, "Tier One" consists only of my sister, cousin, and sister-in-law. These are the women closest to me that I want to make the greatest effort with. These three women are in my life for the long haul, so it made sense to prioritize them over all others. Your "Tier One" may include a longtime best friend, or even someone you recently met on the playground that you'd like to continue to get to know. Whoever these individuals are in your life, they are the ones you place above all others.

I'll be transparent: I don't want to be perceived as a jerk for admitting this. That said, I can't *not* share how beneficial this exercise has been for me. It's not that the women in Tier Three no longer "served" me, so I no longer "served" them. It's more that I constantly felt like I was playing catch-up when I saw them. There wasn't enough regular contact with these people for me to feel like I could deeply invest in them.

For me, minimalism places a strong emphasis on intentionality, and if I was being honest with myself, attempting to cultivate friendships with so many women was no longer possible. In the days before marriage and kids, sure. But as mothers, we have to recognize that there's only so much time in our week. Not to mention, once our children start full-time school, we're even more limited in the time we have to spend with others.

I was tired of just playing catch-up all the time. When you aren't seeing someone regularly, it feels like more of a surface level relationship, and I knew that wasn't what I wanted.

FOR MENTAL HEALTH

Approaching motherhood with a minimalist mindset has made a world of difference in not only the physical clutter in our home, but the mental and emotional clutter of my mind as well.

I am in no way suggesting that minimalism is a cure all for mental health issues, but it can lessen the burden. We care for everything we bring into our homes. It doesn't matter if that simply means storing things in boxes in our basement or dusting them once a week on our knickknack shelf. They not only have a place in our homes, but they also take up precious space in our minds. By owning less, I've been able to focus on the things I enjoy: my children, hobbies, and relationships, all of which benefit my mental health.

> Are you missing out on time with your children because you're spending too much time focusing on household work, specifically clutter and messes?

Mindfulness

Do you ever feel as if you're living on autopilot? You know the feeling: you get into your car at work only to arrive home in your driveway without remembering any of the curves and turns that got you there. While there is scientific reasoning behind this sense of autopilot (scientifically called default mode network), being in this state is not always to our advantage. We're experiencing mindlessness.

I can think of a handful of examples when it's important that our brains react this way: brushing our teeth, typing on a computer, or cooking a typical Monday night meal. But how about when it comes to hours consuming social media? What about that third, fourth, even fifth cookie we've eaten? Or that pile on your kitchen counter that is growing bigger and bigger?

What if, instead of remaining on autopilot, we chose to be mindful?

According to Mindful.org:

> *"Mindfulness is the basic human ability to be fully present, aware of where we are and what we're doing, and not overly reactive or overwhelmed by what's going on around us. Mindfulness is a quality that every human being already possesses, it's not something you have to conjure up, you just have to learn how to access it."*

Practicing mindfulness doesn't mean an action will always follow, it just means you're *aware* of what you're doing. At the time of writing of this book, I still struggle to maintain mindfulness. Writing a book is no small feat, and juggling the emergence of COVID, our current political climate, and attempting to work from home, all while bringing up three children, is *hard*. So I get it. You may have children, a full-time job, maybe even a sick family member to care for, so it can be tough to be mindful.

All that to say, when you create the foundation to practice mindfulness, you can always return. I'll give you an example: I've decluttered my home and made intentional decisions on where to invest my time and money. Regardless of circumstances, I've set myself up with the ability to access it.

I've stated before that my mind reflects the state of my home. A cluttered and messy space equals a mind pulled in many directions. Just think about the amount of time you spend cleaning up the countless toys in your child's room. Wouldn't that time be best spent *with* your child? It's not to say that you won't spend time cleaning up as a mom—of course you will. What I'm suggesting is that amount of overwhelm has a negative effect on your mood. Kim John Payne, author of *Simplicity Parenting*, put it this way:

"Yet simplification is not just about taking things away. It is about making room, creating space in your life, your intentions, and your heart. With less physical and mental clutter, your attention expands, and your awareness deepens...."

When you move from room to room cleaning up and never feeling caught up, it affects your mood.

Everyone has the capability of being mindful. It's a muscle to be strengthened.

> I'd love to see your family's decluttering process in action! Use the hashtag #minimalistmoms on Instagram to share your progress with our community.

CREATION OF THE PODCAST

In 2016, I co-created the *Minimalist Moms Podcast*. What
started as a creative endeavor turned into more of a passion
project. Minimalism was something that impacted my life
immensely and I wanted to explore this concept in regard to
family, from the perspective of motherhood.

One afternoon, I was scrolling through social media and
happened upon a blog post written by an acquaintance from
church. The post detailed her goals for each month of the year,
and her desire for June was to start a podcast. I decided to
reach out, as I'd tossed around the idea of starting one as well.
We brainstormed over drinks a few days after our initial phone

call. The question on the table: what would we talk about? What did we have in common? Well, we were both mothers that prioritized living simply, despite it looking different in both of our lives. A light bulb went off and we aligned on minimalism.

While our minimalist perspectives were very different—she lived in a 3,600 square-foot home and I was living in 800 square feet—we figured the contrast would be one we could use to our advantage. We aspired to have conversations on how we could improve and challenge each other. It wouldn't look the same in each of our lives, but that was a *good* thing.

Flash forward to a handful of weeks after that initial conversation and the *Minimalist Moms Podcast* was set to go. The idea for our first episode wasn't anything too deep, just a "getting to know you" of sorts. I'll be honest, when there was a fancy microphone set before me, I felt odd acting as though we had an audience. At that point, the only people listening were our spouses. But despite the initial hesitance, we continued on for the next couple of years. We explored topics such as when minimalism feels debilitating (a topic near and dear to my heart as I was constantly toeing the line of being a bit frigid when it came to how much I liked to pare down), zero-waste living, clutter zones, "mom style, simplified," and minimalist meal planning. My co-host would brainstorm and create an outline one week, and I would do the same the next. The back and forth allowed us the opportunity to dive into topics we found interesting, while allowing the (sometimes) opposite perspective to speak on the matter, too.

We continued on this trajectory for the next two years, and in late 2018, it was decided that I would take over the podcast reins. My co-host had received a job offer and could no longer dedicate the time needed to the podcast. Our final interview together was with author and well-known minimalist Joshua Becker. While it was sad to close the chapter of our collaboration, it gave me the opportunity to see what I wanted the *Minimalist Moms Podcast* to become in the future.

I knew I didn't want to stop creating altogether, but I wasn't exactly sure what the content would look like moving forward. The thing about having a co-host is that there's always someone to bounce ideas off and engage in witty banter with while recording. It makes for a more genuine production, and that was something I didn't want to lack in the upcoming episodes.

I decided to release my first solo episode, consisting of a mantra and reflection, in January of 2019. The episode went live and was well-received. As I began to write out my process for the future, I found out I was pregnant with our third child. My plans came to an abrupt halt, as I could barely function through my nausea while parenting my other two children, let alone create content for a podcast.

After the first trimester passed, I was back to (somewhat) normal and began to reach out to individuals in the realm of minimalism. One of my first guest interviews was notable zero-waste pioneer Bea Johnson. I couldn't believe she agreed to come on the show. Month after month, I continued to take risks in reaching out to authors, creators, or their publicists, and it surprisingly paid off! I scored another interview with Gretchen Rubin, author and creator of the Four Tendencies framework. The podcast continued to take off from there.

My goal with the podcast is to offer listeners a variety of voices on all kinds of topics within the minimalism/simple living community. It's so important to me to provide a flood of information for listeners to sort through as they craft the simple life that works best for their individual families. The catchphrase of the podcast has always been "think more and do with less." My desire is for listeners to use my resource as a starting point, but also as continual support in their minimalist pursuits.

At the time of this writing, I have been successfully producing the podcast on my own for eighteen months. I've experienced ups and downs with technology and feedback. The one thing that has remained the same is the amazing listeners, who have been encouraging since that first episode. Support and encouragement are what push me to continue to generate content that benefits others as they pursue their own minimalist journeys. I'm not sure when I'll finally close the door on this period of time, but I will say that whenever that time comes, I'll be so grateful to have had the opportunity to speak to so many women—specifically moms—about minimalism.

WHY WE'RE BECOMING MINIMALISTS

So you've read about my background and how I arrived here, but what's in it for you? Why would anyone become a minimalist, especially a minimalist mom? I'll preface my answer by saying that it's only for you to decide. My words will only have so much sway. It won't be until you experience the freedom of living with less that you truly understand the "why" behind it all.

Every one of us makes seemingly insignificant decisions every day that impact the amount of peace or stress in our lives. If accumulating items hasn't made you happy, why don't you try the opposite and start de-ccumulating? (Okay, that's not a word, but you get where I'm going here.) As you de-ccumulate (or declutter) the items in your home, you won't feel the weight of clutter that was once pervasive. I'd be willing to bet that even if you don't feel like you need to massively overhaul your possessions, a good decluttering may be in order. Heck, I'm almost ten years into this minimalist journey of mine and I'm still finding that I need to regularly declutter the things in my home.

MINIMALISM'S EFFECTS ON MOTHERHOOD

As mothers, we want to give our children an idyllic childhood. But who ever said that had to come with bins of toys? So many parents live with the mentality of "It's my child's world and I'm just living in it." Our goal isn't to rid our homes of all toys, creating a farce for anyone who ever stops by. It's about taking back control of what you've allowed to become a bit disordered. That's all. A positive childhood experience isn't dependent on the amount of toys they're gifted, it's more about the relationships you've created with them. (Hey, having a tidy/organized house does wonders for my ability to focus on my children.)

Before we go any further, I'd like to provide you with a few facts regarding our homes these days. In the United States, researchers have found that we have what are called "child-centered homes." The findings show that children's belongings tend to spill out into common areas such as living rooms, dining rooms, kitchens, and even parents' bedrooms. We simply have too much.

What could be contributing to this overabundance of stuff? Well, one perspective is that, as parents spend more time working, they also spend more time purchasing possessions to maintain their quality of life. There is a guilt associated with the lack of time parents spend with their children, so they provide things to make up for it.

Another perspective is the consumer culture we've created. Even before our child is resting comfortably in our arms, we're bombarded by companies trying to sell us stuff for them. If we're not conscientious, we can easily get bogged down by possessions and subscriptions we don't actually need. The problem is that people are trying to use this moment in our lives to capture us as customers. You're told you *need* this and that, and in a state of new beginnings, you believe it. Why question it? This is just what mothers do.

I encourage new mothers (or mothers that plan on having another child) to step back and consider this fact: when you simplify and take everything back to basics, you resist reacting to advertising. This mindset has been extremely beneficial to both me and my children. Simplify. Basics. Don't allow yourself to be led around by opportunistic people who are trying to take advantage of your being a first-time mom.

In a study done by UCLA, mothers are specifically quoted saying that the messier their homes are, the more stressed they feel. I'm sure you can relate. Even living a minimalist lifestyle, there are days when the mess is less than manageable, and it weighs on me. My aim is to reset at naptime and once again after the kids are in bed. When this doesn't happen, it most definitely has a negative effect on my mood.

Consider the area that's currently the most stressful in your life. If you could simplify that one area, it would likely bleed over and simplify everything else. It can be easy to get sucked into the idea that little time-saving hacks can make a large impact, but sometimes doing one big thing can be much more effective. I'm telling you that when it comes to simplifying your life, you will not turn back. I find that moving toward the areas of my life I can control has the biggest impact. There will always be things that are out of your control, so why not take charge of the things you can?

There is a price to pay for every single item that's stored in your home. Take small steps every day and eventually you'll get there. Each small step counts and brings you closer to your end goal.

If you're someone who's on the fence about diving into this lifestyle, let me try to persuade you with some of the reasons that have motivated this shift in my life. One of the biggest takeaways I've found on my journey is that material possessions never satisfy. There's always the desire for more. Want to know why? Because you are being specifically targeted by marketers. The entire job of someone in marketing is to sell to the consumer, to make you feel as though you don't have the latest and greatest. They want you to feel like you aren't "on trend." That you need [fill in the blank] to be like everyone else. Lies.

A mindset I try to maintain whenever I start down the road of "not enough" is this: if I want this in three weeks, I'll buy it. If not, I won't have wasted the money. Try to remember that if it doesn't add to your life, maybe it doesn't belong in your life. The cycle ends when you decide to notice, question, and set boundaries for your purchases and lifestyle.

I can't end this section without also discussing the health benefits associated with decluttering your home. As you begin to declutter, you'll notice a lightness that you hadn't been privy to before. Often, we carry the weight of too many possessions and cluttered homes without recognizing how stressful living in this state can be. Clutter draws our attention away from what our focus should be on. As fellow mothers, I can assume that you take great pride in motherhood. You want to be at your very best for your children, and I assume that you try to combat whatever it is that may be taking time away from them. Have you ever stopped to consider that an overcrowded home may be to blame for your lack of energy (both physical and mental) for your children?

As I go about my day, I have a plethora of choices to make. Attempting to streamline as many decisions as possible is much easier when I don't have to make any regarding clutter. Clutter constantly reminds our brains that we have a huge to-do list. We don't need that kind of distraction.

Why We're Becoming Minimalists

Maybe you're someone who does better with a bulleted list, so here are some of the most important thoughts to consider when it comes to clutter:

- Clutter makes relaxing difficult.
- Clutter draws our attention away from what our focus should be on.
- Clutter causes anxiety because the idea of getting organized is daunting, and the process is seemingly unending.
- Clutter over stimulates our system, causing all of our senses to be on alert.
- Clutter makes daily decision-making difficult, as it's often a reminder of things left undone.
- Clutter causes feelings of embarrassment and may even keep us from hosting gatherings in our homes.
- Clutter frustrates us, as it often contributes to losing important possessions (keys, wallet, phone, headphones, etc.).

By now, my hope is that you see the trickle-down effect that clutter has on every area of life. Plainly put, clutter is unnecessary and can be controlled. I want you to feel empowered to make a change in this area. You can get control over your possessions. You don't have to own all of this stuff.

What will minimalism look like for your family? How many dishes will you own? How many stuffed animals are too many? Will you sell a car and live with only one? Can you condense your wardrobe to only what's necessary?

Though these questions are understandable, the answers don't really matter. Whatever your motivation is to declutter, just start. There is no perfect way to minimize. The only disservice you may do to yourself is choosing not to begin. It may take some time, but don't stall because you're afraid of how long it'll take. Time will pass regardless of whether or not you decide to simplify.

Perhaps you're looking at your home and wondering where to start or how long it will take. Don't feel discouraged if you have a wide variety of possessions to sort through—we collect

things without even noticing. Anthony Graesch, assistant professor of anthropology at Connecticut College, once stated, "I don't think Americans intend to collect so much, but we're really bad at ridding our homes of old possessions before buying new stuff."

Don't discount the process. You don't have to have your house completely decluttered in order to reap the benefits of minimizing your space. This book is now in your hands because you've noticed and are willing to make changes.

BECOMING A MINIMALIST MOM

Brainstorm: Why would the pursuit of minimalism benefit you?

_____

_____

_____

_____

_____

_____

_____

_____

What benefits would you experience by simplifying
your home?

_____

_____

_____

_____

_____

_____

_____

_____

_____

Where will you start?

_____

_____

_____

_____

_____

_____

_____

_____

How will you implement these changes with regard to
your children?

_____

_____

_____

_____

_____

_____

_____

_____

What steps can you take with your spouse or partner
to make sure you stay on top of the decision to live
with less?

_____

_____

_____

_____

_____

_____

_____

_____

_____

AREA OF FOCUS: MINIMIZING POSSESSIONS & INTENTIONAL PURCHASING

The Labor of Physical Decluttering

BORROW, DON'T BUY

I'm not exactly sure how it happened, but I misplaced our ExerSaucer. You know, that giant toy that your growing baby bounces in? Having somehow misplaced this not-so-inconspicuous object, I considered buying another. *My baby needs it*, I thought. I was tempted to buy a new one, but in addition to hesitation over the price tag, I preferred the older model we had. I pulled up the site of one of those comically overpriced infant stores on my laptop (I won't name names, but nod if you know). But then I thought, *why buy when I can borrow?*

So I sent out a message to friends via Facebook instead, and within minutes, several girlfriends had offered me theirs to

borrow. Within twenty-four hours, my baby boy was bouncing away in a borrowed ExerSaucer. No, it may not have been the latest model, but his sweet smile told me he wasn't too concerned with that minor detail.

Looking back, it saddens me to think about all the money I once thought was worth spending in these types of situations. From personal experience, it's best to shoot a message to a girlfriend before investing in something you haven't quite thought through. New toys for your daughter? Why not check with your neighbor to see if you could swap dolls for a week or so? What about that upcoming wedding or special event? Borrow a dress from a girlfriend, don't waste money on one you don't plan on wearing again. That juicer you've been considering? Get the word out and see if someone can loan you theirs while you decide if it's worth the investment. Hey, maybe you can even walk next door and borrow a cup of sugar—you may strike up a friendship you wouldn't have had otherwise.

People that know me personally know that I value intentionality when it comes to spending. There is a vast difference between wants and needs, and it's important to reflect on that. Next time you're contemplating a purchase, consider borrowing it instead.

 MINIMALIST MOM ACTION STEP: Think about something you've been needing to purchase. Is there a possibility that

Area of Focus: Minimizing Possessions & Intentional Purchasing

you could borrow it instead? It's as simple as crafting a post for social media or calling a family member to ask for help.

QUALITY OVER QUANTITY

Let me take you back ten years. I had just entered my twenties. I was making a decent wage (at least I *thought* I was) and believed that with that money, I could justify the purchase of several new blouses for work. I spent every Saturday the same way: sorting through rack after rack at a nearby mall, buying what I believed to be another trendy outfit I just had to have for my upcoming work week. By Wednesday morning, I would find myself yelling to my roommate about having nothing to wear and asking if she would lend me something.

Looking back, I can see that I was struggling from what we now refer to as decision fatigue. Despite having a walk-in closet filled with clothes, I was overwhelmed with the choices. And having already worn my new clothes by midweek, I was desperate for Saturday afternoon to roll around so I could purchase more.

We've heard it before: decision fatigue complicates our lives in an unnecessary manner. Why have an abundance of choices when you can have one choice (or in the case of my closet, limited choices)? After years of creating a life of quantity, I finally shifted my perspective to seeing the value of quality.

Admittedly, a quality product will cost more, but in the long run will cost less than buying multiple, cheaper replacements.

Have you ever stopped to consider the meaning of the popular phrase "quality over quantity"? Quantity is, by definition, "a considerable amount or number" of something. While in a previous life, the number of possessions I owned may have sounded appealing, now I can see how burdensome it was. The decision fatigue, the sorting—it took a toll on me. A very basic explanation of buying quality over quantity is purchasing exactly what you want without spending more on cheap substitutes.

Yes, change can be daunting, and diving into the unknown is often overwhelming. But change also allows you to challenge yourself and learn more about what you like and dislike.

The benefits of maintaining a perspective of quality over quantity encompass more than just material possessions. As a part-time working mother of three, I must be intentional about the time I spend in every facet of life. Gone are the days when my best friend and I met up four times a week. This means that when I do see her, I place that much more importance on being on time, keeping my phone tucked into my purse, and actively listening and engaging. I want to make the most of our time together. I want our experience to be one of high quality.

As a photographer, I can either book six mini sessions in an hour or three full ones, allowing myself to spend more

Area of Focus: Minimizing Possessions & Intentional Purchasing

time focusing on those fewer families. While I may raise my prices to compensate, I'm able to give a high-quality product in return.

This idea can be applied to our relationships, businesses, creative projects, closets, appliances, and even time spent with our children. On your journey to minimize, don't forget to prioritize quality over quantity.

 MINIMALIST MOM ACTION STEP: Is there an area of your life that could benefit from a "quality over quantity" approach? Choose an area: clothing, appliances, makeup, tools, whatever may need tending to. Rid your life of low-quality multiples and keep only what's best.

EVERYTHING HAS A PLACE

Are you familiar with the quote, "A place for everything, and everything in its place"? Maybe you've heard it before but didn't attribute it to him. I know that I first heard the phrase without knowing its origins, but I do appreciate the proverbial nature of it. I like to think that everything should have a "home" of sorts and be stored there when not in use. It's simply about being well-organized, right? Life works better when you know where things can be found, when *everything* has a place.

When everything has a proper place in your home, it eliminates the time we spend looking for lost items. Need new batteries? Those are in the cabinet next to the stairs. Need

to move your partner's car? The keys are hanging next to the light switch near the garage door.

You see where I'm going with this.

When our possessions lack a space to call home, it's likely that they'll end up misplaced at some point or another. Think of it as not only providing order in your home, but also in your mind.

As minimalists, our goal is to cultivate the spaces that work for our lifestyle. We won't receive the benefit of extra time on our schedule if we're constantly trying to configure what is lost or has no home. A lot of us don't get rid of clutter; rather, we move it around our homes from place to place. This is just another habit that keeps us stuck. Take the time to really think

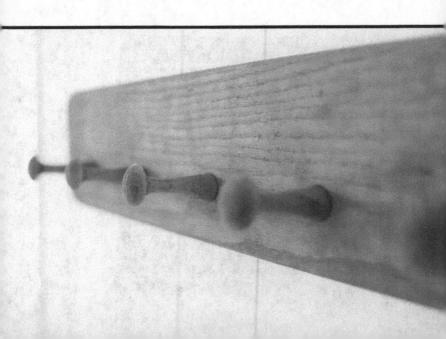

through where your items belong. Don't just give them a home "for now"—this mentality only keeps you stuck!

Get yourself into the habit of regularly putting your possessions back where they belong. After you use the television remote, put it back on the side table so it doesn't become lodged in your couch cushions. When you use the vacuum cleaner, place it back in the hallway closet so it's not cluttering up your living room or hallway. Remember that clutter hinders our mental capacity. Making the time to do a ten- to twenty-minute "tidy" each day will put your home back in order so that you can begin the next morning fresh and organized. You'll wake to find everything has a place, ready to begin the day anew.

 MINIMALIST MOM ACTION STEP: To begin, look around the room you're currently sitting in—what is out of place? A hoodie on the ground? The remote control? A credit card on the counter? Whatever it may be, put it back in its place. What about the things you notice that don't have a home? It's time to deal with them. Create or find a home, or else it's time to toss 'em. Continue to do this through the various rooms in your home. Do it daily. It'll become second nature, and noticing these things will just become a part of your regular tidying routine.

Area of Focus: Minimizing Possessions & Intentional Purchasing

ONE IS ENOUGH

How often do you find yourself in a situation where you've treated yourself to more than one of something, only to be left with a less than satisfactory experience?

This has been more than true for me when, for example, it comes to that second piece of cake at a birthday party. However, what does it look like when you apply it to your clothing purchases? Your accessories? Your groceries?

You might have the mindset that if one is good, more will be better. But what happens when more *isn't* better, when just one would have sufficed?

Let's be honest, who among us hasn't been tempted by a "buy one, get one" sale? Typically, we see this deal and focus on one word: free. We receive two sweaters for the price of one— who wouldn't jump on board? Yet, as you gain perspective, you can see it for what it is: an appealing marketing ploy.

Marketers attempt to convince the consumer that they need this deal. What ends up happening is that the prices of both items are built into the initial purchase. We aren't really getting anything for free, we're just getting two inexpensive items sold at a markup for one.

Marketers try to make you crave more so they can make a profit. They dangle a catchy deal, and the tactic usually works, regardless if the product is something you need. The problem is that when you purchase that one, it's then easier to say "yes" to more. You're already in the mindset of desire. But I challenge you to consider in that moment if the first purchase was one you even wanted to make in the first place. Was it premeditated, or was it a spur of the moment decision? When we are spontaneous with our purchases, we often find ourselves regretting them.

Going back to the food analogy (because those typically work well for me, so I'm hoping to paint a picture for you, too): I was at a book club meeting and someone brought delicious cupcakes from a local bakery. These cupcakes are known for

being the best in Columbus, but I couldn't decide if I wanted to indulge. As I sat there staring, a friend suggested we split one, and I couldn't resist! I enjoyed every last bite of vanilla bean glaze, but I had a pull for more. We decided to split another one, and as you may have guessed, it was the wrong move. One was enough. I was in sugar overload. My stomach hurt and I regretted my decision almost immediately. I savored that first half, but the second was less enjoyable.

If you own only one of something, aren't you more likely to take better care of it? Will you savor your first cupcake serving instead of mindlessly consuming another? The majority of the time, the answer is that one is sufficient. One is enough.

 MINIMALIST MOM ACTION STEP: In what area do you tend to over-indulge? Where do you take more than one? Do you typically regret the decision? Be honest with yourself. Moving forward, make changes as you see fit and use this as a push to rid your home of multiples you no longer need.

IF EVERYTHING IS YOUR FAVORITE, NOTHING IS YOUR FAVORITE

"If everything is your favorite, nothing is your favorite." This is something I regularly tell my daughter, specifically because she likes to hoard her possessions in her room. She says she doesn't want to share with her brother or cousin because, "It's my favorite toy, mom!"

I repeatedly have to remind her that for something to be her "favorite," it has to stand alone. Of course, we can have a handful of favorite things. However, placing that label on *all* her toys devalues each of them.

In a desire to prove my point further, I picked up a dictionary to define the term "favorite." The simple definition according to Merriam-Webster is "one that is treated or regarded with special favor or liking."

Now consider, what possessions in your life receive preferential treatment? Are you calling several items your favorites because you don't know how to purge your space of clothes? Tools? Books? Movies? Equipment?

Over time, our favorites can shift, but it's important that we limit our favorites to make sure they're prioritized.

Author Karen Martin has a similar idea with regard to what we prioritize in our lives. In her book *The Outstanding Organization*, she writes, "When everything is a priority, nothing is a priority." If priority is defined as "a thing that is regarded as more important than others," we then need to apply this to the way we regard our possessions. Which of our possessions are more important than the others? You may have to get brutally honest or invite someone over to help as you navigate and narrow down your favorite items.

Area of Focus: Minimizing Possessions & Intentional Purchasing

Again, I think that as adults, we may have a couple of favorites. But it's unlikely that your twenty pairs of shoes are all favorites. Which ones do you wear? Which ones do you save for only certain occasions once a year? Maybe it's time to rid yourself of some and elevate others.

It's important to be a leader in this area. Your children are watching and learning to navigate their own understanding of favorites—what to keep, and how tight to hold on to their possessions. How can you expect your child to choose a favorite when you're unable to make the decision for yourself?

As you begin to purge "favorites" from your life, ask yourself these questions: Is it really my favorite? Can I go without it? I challenge you to address this "favorite" mentality. It's an easy behavior to slip into, but it's time to purge superfluous

possessions. Remember: If everything is your favorite, nothing is your favorite.

 MINIMALIST MOM ACTION STEP: Are you able to pinpoint your favorite things? If not, why is that? Is it because there may be too many to count? I can tell you what a couple of mine are: my scrapbooks, AirPods, and mid-century modern hutch. Those are my favorite things. I've detached from my other possessions—this doesn't mean I wouldn't be sad to see them go, but I can most definitely go without them. Make a list of your favorite items. It's okay if you have a handful. The problem occurs when everything seems to be a "favorite"...

NEED LESS

As I've previously hinted, in my early twenties I was what you'd consider a compulsive spender. The more I could fill up my closet, the happier I was (or so I thought). Consumerism tends to be a negative cycle: a shopping high leads to a feeling of unfulfillment shortly after, and it repeats.

What I've learned throughout my minimalist journey is the importance of intentionality with purchases. Not only does it save money, but it allows us to curate spaces that truly represent ourselves, as opposed to what marketers are tempting us with each time we step into Target.

Nowadays, if there's something I "want," I record it on my phone's list app and wait (at minimum) two weeks. If that item is still something I think about by then, I'll go ahead and allow myself to buy it. More often than not, however, I forget about it because it wasn't necessary to begin with! With that said, don't forget to ask yourself:

- Do I love it?
- Do I have something similar?
- Will I use it often?
- Do I really *need* it?

Be honest with yourself: how often do you find yourself using the word "need"? Go ahead and start to think about how you use it in your day-to-day life. Seriously, stop reading, go and

grab a pen and paper, and track your "needs" for one week. I think you'll be surprised …

One week later…

Alright, what did you notice? I'd be willing to bet that you'll see similar "needs" on your list: I need a new television. My child needs a new computer game. My living room needs new artwork. I need to upgrade my iPhone.

Need, by definition, is to "require (something) because it is essential or very important." As minimalists, we're still going to want things (we're only human, after all), so don't consider yourself a failure if you happen to make an unintended purchase. Instead, use it as another reminder to notice your impulses. We're hardwired to take the bait of new and shiny purchases. However, when we take the time to step away and take inventory of what we *want*, we may realize that we don't *need* anything at all. This new approach to buying may seem overthought, but the more you practice intentional spending, the easier it becomes. Need less.

 MINIMALIST MOM ACTION STEP: What items are floating around your mind that you've been thinking about purchasing? Write those items down. Return in a couple of weeks. Are they still items you need? Maybe so. More often than not, you'll be just fine without them.

USE IT UP

I started writing this area of focus from the basic perspective that it's important to "use up" household items. My thought was to stop hoarding perfumes, shoes, items of clothing, candles, and food. However, the longer I sat with the idea, the more I realized that it's a fairly straightforward concept. The idea of "using up" is nothing new to a minimalist. My objective, then, is for *you* to experience the freedom that comes from using things up that have been forgotten. In my house, I've found this to be clear when it comes to my kitchen.

Like most people during the COVID-19 pandemic, my husband and I were forced to get creative when it came to cooking meals. That can of beans that had been pushed to the back of

the pantry? Use it up! The fifty-pound bag of flour in the basement? Bread for everyone, use it up! The frozen bananas in the freezer? Smoothies for breakfast, use 'em up!

You see where I'm going here. In using up the items in our pantry, we have fundamentally changed how we interact with our kitchen. We've changed the way we think about food and have become more creative. Gone are the days when we made multiple trips to the grocery store each week. We use what we have and build our list from there. It's provided for a more versatile mix of ingredients when we can pair something with what we already have at home.

Can you think of an example in your own life that would force you to "use it up"? What's keeping you from doing so? Maybe the item was expensive. Maybe it was one of a kind. Maybe it was too pretty. Whatever your reasoning may be, the "hoarding" of these items only wastes storage, money, and time.

Let me provide one last example. I once received a lovely organic candle for my birthday. I knew the candle was likely a bit pricey, so I wanted to burn it only on special occasions. The problem was there never seemed to be an occasion special enough to burn it. It remained on my shelf, dusty and unused.

Don't allow your hoarding tendencies to follow you into motherhood. It's easy to store up craft supplies, markers, and colored pencils. I can relate to being one of those moms who

— 77 —

wants craft time to be organized and efficient. But when I stay in this mindset, nothing ever gets used.

There is nothing sadder than unused, forgotten items taking up space in your home. Use it up!

 <u>**MINIMALIST MOM ACTION STEP:**</u> What items do you currently own that need to be used up? Brainstorm how you could put these items to good use. If need be, think outside the box! It's fun to use things up.

FREE STUFF IS STILL STUFF

When I was a girl, I absolutely loved to browse garage sales. (I'll be honest, I still do, but rarely find time to go.) On summer

Saturday mornings, I'd set off with a few dollars in my pocket in search of a good deal. For some reason, I absolutely loved looking through the piles of possessions that people no longer wanted. I would stumble upon the most bizarre items—it felt like a treasure hunt. As I walked through the garages or driveways, my eyes would be on alert for the four-letter word I hoped to see most: F-R-E-E.

There was one time in particular that I remember seeing that word above a bin of stuffed animals. Bingo! I'm slightly embarrassed to admit this to you, but I loaded up my bicycle basket, arms, and bookbag with as many animals as would fit. They were free, after all.

I remember getting home and unloading my haul when my mom caught sight of me through the front door. She challenged me on why I found it necessary to bring home six or so new stuffed animals when I already had more than my fair share upstairs. I'm sure I argued that they were free, but I can't remember much more of the interaction than that.

You may be curious as to why I'm recounting this story to you, and here is my answer: free stuff is still stuff. My mom was right to challenge me, the conversation just needed to move one step further. I did have a bed full of stuffed animals in my room that added to the clutter and excess in our home. By bringing in more animals—free or not—I was contributing to the load of the household.

Area of Focus: Minimizing Possessions & Intentional Purchasing

Just because something is free, doesn't mean it won't cost you. It may end up costing you in time spent cleaning up or around said item. It may end up costing you attention to maintain it, too. These are valuable resources—especially in motherhood. As a young girl, I wouldn't say that I was aware of this mentality, but it most certainly affected my parents (whether or not they were privy to it).

What does it say when a person sets out a box of free stuffed animals in their garage? If they weren't valued enough for the original owner to make a profit off them, maybe I should have reconsidered my desire to obtain them for myself. What that person was implying with their decision to set out the box was, "I don't value or want these items anymore." Sure, one person's junk is another person's treasure, but sometimes one person's junk is just another person's junk.

Leave behind the free pens, roadside "treasures," and stuffed animals. Don't indulge in a buy one, get one deal if you're unlikely to ever need two of the same shirt (even if it comes in two colors you love). Walk away! Free stuff is still stuff. Your time and attention are too valuable to waste on things you don't need (or want) in the first place.

 MINIMALIST MOM ACTION STEP: Do you tend to bring free stuff into your home? Where are you storing it? Do you really need it? The next time you're at a conference, the doctor's office, the bank, a garage sale, or wherever else you may be handed free stuff, politely say "no, thank you."

LESS STUFF, MORE SPACE

We all experience moments in our lives when we feel like we need to upgrade. There are a couple of individuals in my life that regularly want to move homes so they'll have more space to spread out or store more "stuff." While I'm not opposed to moving if you truly do need the space, I'd like to challenge this idea.

What if instead of more space, we had less stuff?

Instead of looking to purchase more space in a home or apartment, focus your energy on condensing your possessions to provide you the space you need. I challenge you to conjure an image of your current residence prior to moving in. Do you remember how much space you felt you had as you completed the final walk-through? As you moved and settled in, the rooms slowly began to fill up. A chair here, a shelf there. A woven basket here, a bench there. On and on it continues, until you feel like you have no space.

Did it ever occur to you that maybe it wasn't the home that was the problem, but simply the number of things keeping you from really experiencing the space you purchased? It's time for you to stop thinking of the lack of space as the problem. I'm willing to bet that you have enough space to live comfortably—it's your possessions taking up room.

Area of Focus: Minimizing Possessions & Intentional Purchasing

Have you ever looked at one of those heat maps that trace human activity in the home? A study done by UCLA shows that possessions, when we allow them to dominate our homes, take up our time and resources. The study suggests that square footage in the dining room and porch areas is wasted, as people tend to gather around the kitchen and the television. Author Steve Adcock says, "The findings were not pretty. In fact, they helped prove how little we use our big homes for things other than clutter...most families don't use large areas of their homes—which means they've essentially wasted money on space they do not need."

We fill our homes with more and more consumer goods and convince ourselves that we really do need all that space. We have more stuff than we know what to do with. But instead of

looking at your home and immediately plotting your next trip to Ikea, think about what needs to come out. What is hanging on your walls that should come down?

Don't build your home around visual appeal, but rather around functionality. Look for redundant spaces (the spaces that serve the same purpose in your home). For example, your kids' "study room" is useless if they always do their homework at the kitchen table; this room can be used for something else. We're looking for space in our home that we've otherwise filled with clutter. Create space in your home by first owning less.

 MINIMALIST MOM ACTION STEP: I highly recommend reading through the book *Cozy Minimalist Home: More Style, Less Stuff*, by Myquillyn Smith. She walks you through the process of decorating your home without using extra resources, time, and money.

THINK TWICE

Unless you've been, as they say, "living under a rock" for the last five years, you've likely heard of author and famous organizer Marie Kondo. Kondo is known for her decluttering method that encourages people to consider whether each of their possessions "sparks joy." When using this approach, I think we can summarize it further by asking ourselves two things: 1) Do I want this item? and 2) Where is its home?

Area of Focus: Minimizing Possessions & Intentional Purchasing

In Kondo's words, she suggests, "The best way to choose what to keep and what to throw away is to take each item in one's hand and ask: 'Does this spark joy?' If it does, keep it. If not, dispose of it. This is not only the simplest but also the most accurate yardstick by which to judge."

Decluttering can quickly become an overwhelming experience for people. It truly is more mental than physical, so I'm not sure that placing a blanket statement on the process is helpful. It's easy to rid your home of too-small clothes, excess pens, and broken toys, but it can be difficult to navigate whether or not something evokes joy. There are millions of people that have read the book and subscribed to the notion of possessions needing to "spark joy." I, however, want to play a bit of a devil's advocate. As we begin to implement

this process, we're calling on our emotions to guide us—specifically, as I hold this item, is it stirring up joy in me? Emotional decision-making is something I avoid altogether. I'd be willing to argue that we should take the same approach when making decisions about our possessions.

Instead of seeing whether something "sparks joy," what if we challenged our initial reaction and gave it a second thought?

I used to subscribe to Kondo's idea of sparking joy until I had an experience that made me second guess whether the process was best for me. A few months prior to my youngest niece's birth, a very pregnant me sorted through my oldest daughter's baby clothes and tried to decide which items "sparked joy" in me. I kept the ones that did in case the baby inside me were to be a girl, or to pass along to my grandchildren. Flash forward to a couple of months ago, I was sorting through the same bin of clothing and questioning why I kept half of them in the first place. Yes, my daughter looked cute when she wore them several years before, but would *her* children really want to wear them in the 2040s/2050s? I felt so detached from the bin of clothing and decided to give the majority to my sister and donate the rest.

Of course, there were a handful of outfits that "sparked joy" in me. However, my emotions had proven to be fickle. I was in a different headspace nine months prior, and I'll be in a different headspace nine months in the future. When I think twice, it aids in the decluttering of my life. Parting with our belongings isn't simple—it can be very stressful and frustrating. When we consider whether something sparks joy, it's not a foolproof question that will magically clarify the decision-making process. Not every item will spark joy in you. There are items that are useful that make you joyful because of the convenience they provide: your clothes, your appliances, your children's possessions. Some of these things may not bring you joy (so to speak), but even then they make you happy for a variety of other reasons (for example, maybe you're joyful about your daughter's Furby because it brings her happiness, but you wouldn't keep that thing for thirty seconds if it were up to you).

All of that to say, Marie Kondo definitely knows what she's doing when it comes to decluttering. She has sold eleven million copies of her notable book *The Life-Changing Magic of Tidying Up*, has a show on Netflix, and has helped countless individuals purge their homes of excess. My critique isn't with her ability to help others, but simply with the method that may prove faulty for some.

 MINIMALIST MOM ACTION STEP: Are you currently storing possessions that you originally chose to put aside? If so, go back to consider them for a second time. Sort through those items again. Do you feel any different? If you are more detached this time around, get rid of them. If not, place another boundary of time and then sort one more time before making a final decision.

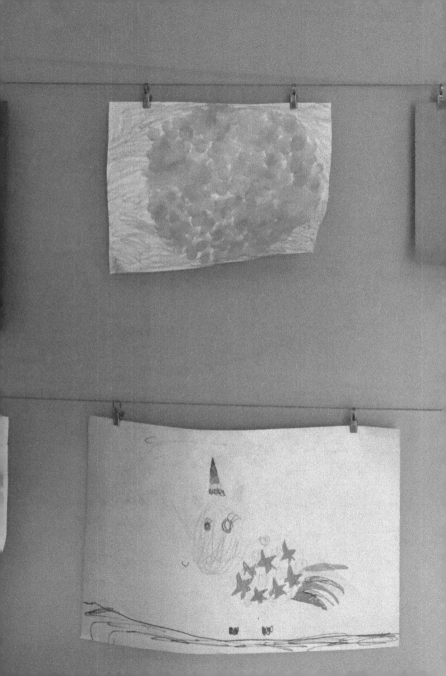

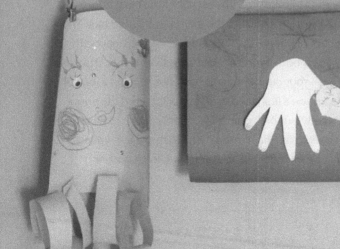

LET'S
SIMPLIFY:
SENTIMENTAL
ITEMS

THE MOST DIFFICULT ITEMS TO DECLUTTER

One of the most difficult questions I receive when giving advice usually comes down to this: how do I minimize sentimental items? You've begun this minimalist journey—you've cleaned out your closet, donated the extra bike, purged your excess coffee mugs—but what about that one in the back? Yeah, that one from college that you never use but continues to take up space in your otherwise tidy cabinet. What about those paintings from your daughter's preschool days? Where are you storing them? These "most important" items are saturated with memories. It's difficult to navigate what to toss, store, and donate. But it is my hope that this section will inspire you to reconsider what you're holding on to tightly and what you may (*may*) be able to part with...

I'll be the first to admit that sentimental items are one of the toughest things to minimize. The reason? It isn't just about the value of the item itself, but the *memory* attached to it. The coffee cup from college, the Cabbage Patch doll (maybe this is just me), the wedding dress. What about items that attach you to others? Your grandmother's costume jewelry, a lock of hair from your son's first haircut, the umbilical cord from your first baby's belly button (again, maybe just me). As minimalist moms, we recognize that our goal isn't to throw everything away, but to be intentional about what we keep, ensuring those items are the most meaningful. I think when considering sentimental items, we have to remember the connection between our brain and the item. The item triggers a memory. Therefore, we become emotionally attached to it. How can we combat this?

> The biggest challenge: find a balance between your past and your present.

What does this mean exactly? It means to appreciate the things you hold on to, but not to create a museum for the things you're choosing to continue to store in boxes. You absolutely can hold on to those special items of your

grandmother's, but if they remain in boxes, can I gently ask you why? Getting down to the reasoning behind why you continue to store these items will make it easier to assess what to get rid of and what to keep.

There are a handful of ways to approach minimizing sentimental possessions. However, there is one that may be the toughest but quickest, and that is: just get rid of it! This option won't work for everyone and every item, but for many, it's best to rip off the Band-Aid quickly and be done with the task. As for those who prefer a slower approach, I have a few suggestions for how to pare down these items. Build momentum by taking small steps. As you gain traction in this area, small "wins" will make it easier to comfortably purge sentimental items throughout your home.

SUGGESTIONS FOR DECLUTTERING SENTIMENTAL ITEMS

My first suggestion is to **recognize sentimentality as an emotion**. Emotional charges can be strong, but we must recognize whether or not the thoughts are rational or helpful. As you begin to process the emotions you're experiencing, I suggest pausing. Take the time to consider what exact emotion is tugging on you. Is it weighty or uplifting? Positive or negative? Consider why you are storing the item. This is what I was talking about in the section above. When we dig into the "why," we may find out that we don't like the feelings associated with the item. Ask yourself one more time: are the feelings positive or negative? And if the answer is the latter, it's time to let go. The weight of keeping the item as well as the negativity attached to it are unnecessary burdens to bear. Letting go will release not only space in your home, but space in your mind.

That brings me to my second suggestion: **make sure the memories attached are good ones.** Don't hold on to stuff out of obligation or guilt. Are you still holding on to items from a past relationship? Maybe you need to let go in order to move forward. Are you someone that usually keeps all photographs? If a particular item induces guilt whenever you see it, the best way to get rid of the guilt is to get rid of the item.

Remember that having the memory is more precious than having the thing. So often, we hold on to a possession because we can't bear to part with the memory associated with it.

A lot of people hold on to items because of the stress associated with having spent money on it in the first place. They don't like the feeling of having "wasted" money by purchasing said item, so they keep it around to justify the money spent. I'm here to tell you that you waste your money when you buy something, not when you get rid of it. **Just do it.** Hold your breath, put it in the trash (for personal items like photos) or donation box (for other items), shut the lid, and drop it off immediately. Later, you won't remember half of what you gave away.

My next piece of advice is to **consult the "experts."** By now, you're probably familiar with Joshua Becker, of *Becoming Minimalist*. In his opinion, we should think about curating our items with care, not using our home as a storeroom. What would this look like practically? I say pick one item to keep (and/or display) and donate the rest. This can be difficult. Here's an example I have from my own family: after my aunt passed away, her Native American ceramic collection was spread among her three siblings. Each of the siblings, including my dad, received a couple of these precious figurines. To this day, my father displays them in his glass cabinet.

Stick to this quote from designer and poet William Morris:

"Have nothing in your house that you do not know to be useful or believe to be beautiful."

For the most part, if it's collecting dust in a box, it's neither useful nor beautiful.

Find a way to use the sentimental items in your everyday life. Do you have a collection of your grandmother's tea cups that remain in a box? Use them! Enjoy a daily teatime with your child, or a weekly or monthly teatime with friends. Don't allow the item to collect dust or go forgotten because you were too hesitant to use it. If the sentimental items don't have a practical purpose—like your grandfather's Mickey Mantle or Babe Ruth baseball cards from the 1960s—you could display them in a shadow box frame. The cards were once important treasures to your grandfather. By displaying them in your office or living room, it'll give you the opportunity to think of the sentiment each time you pass by.

I'll quickly mention this tip, too: you can always **photograph the sentimental item** to preserve the memory. It's a way to look back on the item without having to store it. The space in our homes is precious—and often limited—so this is a great way to take a trip down memory lane without forfeiting otherwise valuable space.

What about the items you're unsure you'll need down the road? My initial response is that you can't predict your future. My next response would be to start slow. Why begin with items that contain sentimental value or emotional attachment? Don't start here! Start with the areas of clutter that surround your day-to-day. Can you enjoy a meal at the dining room table without papers scattered about? Can you easily find the Tupperware or kitchen utensil you need to cook dinner? Gain initial momentum and *then* move toward trickier items. Personally, it has been easier for me to be more decisive because I've been at this for about a decade! I've worked through what is personally important and am able to toss the rest. That said, I can tell you that if you're worried you've purged too many infant clothes or that you'll miss that treasured DVD at some point, you can always find a version of it again. Borrow from friends/family. Utilize Facebook groups, church groups, or parenting groups. Remember that it's better to live day-to-day in a decluttered home than to hold onto things you only "may" need in the future.

Finally, one of the best pieces of advice I can leave you with when it comes to sentimental possessions would be to **set limits**. Don't set such rigid boundaries that you become resentful of minimalism and throw in the towel. That said, don't keep more than you deem necessary. For children, I recommend allowing one container for sentimental items. Things I've put in my daughter's box include her first ballet leotard, a bookmark she was gifted by Belle in Disney World, cards from her first birthday/holidays, and hair from her first haircut. Obviously there are things in this box that will, in the long term, mean more to me than her. That's why it's important to reevaluate the items each time the box is full. I find that this technique also benefits older children as they become collaborators in this decision-making.

SENTIMENTAL CHILDREN'S ITEMS

Artwork

If you have a child like mine, you know that the artwork piles up quicker than you can keep up. It's tricky to know what to keep and what to recycle, so that's why I stick with the

photography tip. This happens in a couple of ways. Whenever artwork is created, I'll ask if she wants it displayed on the refrigerator. We don't completely cover our fridge (one of the biggest clutter accumulators), but I do have six metal clasps where we can attach her latest masterpieces. I switch them out as she continues to create. The super special, top 5 percent of her creations are stored in her memento box (each child has their own box).

For everything else, the photography comes into play: I photograph it with my phone and then toss or recycle it. You see, I make a family scrapbook each year, and I have a section within the book called "Charlotte the Artist" where I include these photos with captions underneath. Now, you don't have to get this detailed—if you'd prefer just to upload everything to one digital album, that's okay, too. Another idea is to use social media: post the artwork to its own private Instagram account (or another appropriate app) that you share with family and friends. Not only will your child enjoy sharing their creations with other loved ones, but the account can serve as a keepsake of sorts. From there, you can easily have it printed through Chatbooks or another similar organization that's connected to social media.

My biggest tip for storing and deciding what artwork to keep is to remember that you cannot keep it all. When debating what stays, ask yourself these questions:

- How much time and effort did my child put into the creation of this piece?
- Does the piece display a stage we'd love to recall in the future?
- Does my child have a strong opinion regarding the piece?

One last reminder: no need to blatantly throw anything away in front of your child's face. Artwork is typically "gifted" to parents, so it's best to be nonchalant and get rid of it discreetly. After your initial artwork purge, your goal is to be sure it never accumulates again. Cultivate the habit of regularly sorting through what stays and what goes.

Baby Clothes

I find this to be the king of sentimental items, at least in my home. It can be tough to purge these because of our emotional attachment to the memories of our children as babies. We fondly look back on the days when our kids were small enough to fit into the tiny clothes we've held on to. I vividly remember my daughter wearing a certain outfit *all* the time. When we begin to declutter this area, it almost feels like we're excavating that moment from our memories.

I have a couple of tips for how to best navigate this area, and my first one would be to ask the simple question: why are you keeping these items of clothing? Do you plan on having more children? If so, go ahead and save the items that aren't worn out or heavily stained, but get rid of the rest. Next: are you saving these because you want to use them as hand-me-downs in the future? I know, I know. There is something special about imagining your future grandchildren in the same clothing your child once wore. But remember to be realistic—your child probably won't start their own family for a minimum of twenty more years. Will they really want their old baby clothes for their children? Maybe the answer is yes, but more likely, the answer is no. It's highly unlikely they'll want to be gifted an entire wardrobe of clothes from their childhood. Allow them the freedom to choose the clothing for their child.

Lastly, instead of keeping baby clothes only to toss them a few years in the future, consider donating them to individuals who will use them right away, while they remain in style. Decluttering baby clothes is a bittersweet part of watching your children grow. If you're feeling extra sentimental, limit yourself to one bin of clothing. No more. Also, as you're sorting through your favorites, think back to the outfits you may have photographed on your child. Some of my favorite outfits still "exist" in old photos that remain dear to me. It's a win-win: I have a tangible memory of my child in the outfit, and I don't have to store said outfit forever.

Pictures

This is so tough. As a photographer, I struggle with wanting to keep a variety of photographs. However, how often do you look back at all seven photos you took of your child blowing bubbles? Typically, we look back and swoon over one or two photos that are the most special. The best way to approach this sentimental item is to get into the habit of sorting through and deleting photos at the end of each day. I'm especially sure to do this on a day where I've taken dozens of pictures. I go through, "heart" my favorites, and proceed to delete the others. It can be difficult to make these choices, but not only will your digital clutter stay minimal, you'll have curated the best of the best photos to print or share. The same concept of favorites could also apply to physical photographs.

Let's Simplify: Sentimental Items

Toys

We all have those handful of toys that are difficult to part with: the doll, the train set, the remote-controlled car, the wagon. It's tough, I get it. Even I admit to feeling heartbroken here and there when the time has come for my child to stop playing with a certain toy they once loved. I'll always think of that scene in *Toy Story 3* when Andy passes Woody down to Bonnie and says, "See you around, partner." (Don't tell me you haven't seen *Toy Story 3?*) The attachment we feel toward our children's toys make sense. They're a representation of our children at a younger, simpler time. If you're finding it too difficult to purge these items, have someone else toss/donate the bag or box for you. That said, if the toy is in good enough condition, you may consider selling it on Facebook

Marketplace or passing it on to someone who will continue to give it love. As with all of these items, I suggest taking pictures of the toys or stuffed animals to make it easier to let them go.

Books

My advice here may surprise you: keep them! What wonderful gifts to pass down to future generations. If the books are in good enough condition, save them for your grandchildren (or other family members) as a way to continue to promote early literacy and a love of reading. My father kept several books from my childhood (I didn't know until I had children of my own), and he uses them for bedtime stories when the kids spend the night. If you find that there are too many to store, choose your favorites and pass the rest along to a child in need. There are many places to donate: local libraries, daycares, children's hospitals, non-profits, and homeless shelters. A quick Google search should provide you with options in your area.

DECLUTTERING SENTIMENTAL POSSESSIONS: WHAT EVERYDAY MINIMALIST MOMS ARE SAYING

Ariane: I like to use an idea from decluttering author Dana K. White: "Whose memory is it? Yours or someone else's?" This has helped with things from my childhood that my mother kept and then gave to me when I had children. Most of it isn't sentimental for me, so I don't need to feel bad about getting rid of it. Also, in Joshua Becker's book *The More of Less: Finding the Life You Want Under Everything You Own*, he says to keep the best! If I know something isn't the best [regarding sentimentality], I don't have to keep it.

Candi: I ask myself, "Does this item still have the sentimental value that it once had?" (along the lines of Marie Kondo's "Does it spark joy?"), and appreciate the purpose it served and the joy it once brought.

Tesha: It may seem strange, but sometimes just thanking the items for the pleasure they brought is enough. Saying goodbye helps me let go of sentimental items.

Emily: For sentimental items, remember that memories aren't found in the items themselves, although it's hard to separate the two. Take a photo and write a story about why each item is meaningful to you. Share the story with a loved one, like your kids or spouse/partner. Then keep only the things that are most meaningful, display them if you can, and bless other people with the rest.

Simran: Artwork is a *hard* one, since everything kids create is so special. Keep your favorite pieces in a scrapbook or dedicated box. Take pictures of the rest, or use them as wrapping paper or cards for the next special occasion.

Elissa: When we were on the move and purging frequently, we simply told the kids, "You know how much this item has blessed you? Now it's time to give it to another child so they can be blessed, too." The kids mostly rolled with it happily when we framed it that way.

Rachel: When I am hesitant to get rid of toys, books, art, etc. that my children no longer use, I take a picture of them holding it. I'm not attached to the item, I'm attached to the memories, and I can recall those memories at any time. The Timehop app is a great reminder of those special times with some of our favorite things, which is way better than storing unused stuff in a box somewhere.

BECOMING A MINIMALIST MOM: SAY GOODBYE TO SENTIMENT

Which item(s) are you having a difficult time
letting go of?

_____

_____

_____

_____

_____

_____

_____

_____

_____

_____

_____

Is the item(s) currently on display or being used
regularly? If you wish to use or display it, list the
item(s) and how you can do so.

_____

_____

_____

_____

_____

_____

_____

_____

_____

_____

What memories might be attached to these item(s),
making it difficult to say goodbye?

_____

_____

_____

_____

_____

_____

_____

_____

_____

Let's Simplify: Sentimental Items

Do the memories bring you down, make you feel sad,
or make you feel guilty?

_____

_____

_____

_____

_____

_____

_____

_____

Brainstorm: How could you preserve the memory of
the item(s) while still letting go?

_____

_____

_____

_____

_____

_____

_____

_____

AREA OF FOCUS: TIME MINIMALISM

Prioritizing, & Reducing Distractions in Your Day

SAY, "HECK YES"

Years ago, I found myself caught in a season of "yes." My people-pleasing heart couldn't bear to turn down the extra opportunity to serve, the new group to lead, or the unforeseen game night. While a full schedule isn't necessarily a bad thing, I realized my hurried acceptance led to a hurried execution. My intentions were good and my heart was in the right place, yet I was left with over-scheduled days and a budding resentment toward all of my responsibilities. Do you ever feel like this, too?

At the time, I knew I needed to address my over-eager personality, but I wondered what would actually work. As I

thought through how to start saying "no," I decided instead to say, "heck yes!"

Stay with me here. We have the ability to commit to or decline any opportunity that comes our way, but when we implement the "heck yes" mentality, we can be confident in saying "yes" to the right things—the things that excite us!

Consider all of the times you've said "yes" to something with a note of hesitation in your voice. In the back of your mind, you're cognizant of this hesitation, but fear persuades you to accept without delay. Why do we do this to each other? More importantly, why do we do this to ourselves?

Anytime you're making a decision about something that affects your time and energy, ask yourself: is this a "heck yes"? If you hesitate, aren't sure, or simply don't feel connected to it, your answer is allowed to be "no." You don't have to do things to please other people. Invest your time in the things that matter most to you. When you do, you'll feel more fulfilled, more relaxed, and you can go to bed knowing that you took control of your time.

This isn't the first time we've spoken on the importance of minimizing your schedule. However, consider this chapter another gesture of encouragement to remember that you don't have to say "yes" to things you aren't excited about.

Author and entrepreneur Derek Sivers says:

> *"Whatever excites you, go do it.*
> *Whatever drains you, stop doing it."*

Of course, there are exceptions to this mindset. Most of us aren't walking into work each day ready to crush our to-do list with a "heck yes." But for all of those extra events, appointments, groups, and schedule compromises, visualize the execution when committing to something. Can you see yourself pulling it off with passion and energy? When I am passionate about something, I see how I can make it happen, because I actually want it to get done. You will experience more joy from beginning to end when you think about the full picture. When you aren't committed to something, it takes time and more energy.

This isn't easy at first. It will take time to trust yourself as you go from over-accepting to only accepting what feels right. When we say "yes" to everything, our schedules become too burdensome to balance. There is only so much time in the day. We must acknowledge our limits and then move forward, prioritizing what's important and exciting to us.

Create space in your life by remembering to say, "heck yes!"

 <u>MINIMALIST MOM ACTION STEP:</u> This month, make all of your responses either a "no" or a "heck yes"!

START TODAY

Ever since I can remember, I've been a procrastinator. I'm not sure if it's the thrill of racing to complete a task, or if I'm just plain terrible at time management. I'm surprisingly organized in other ways, but I regularly struggle with motivation to begin a new endeavor. As I continue to put off what needs to get done, I lose precious time that could be beneficial to the structure of my schedule. Time spent here and there only inhibits my ability for sustained focus.

That said, I've grown quite a bit over the last couple of years, and though it's tough, I remember that there's no time like the present to tackle my goals and to-dos. One example that comes to mind is this book you have in your hands. I always

knew I wanted to write a book, and I wasn't quite sure how it would play out, but I *was* always sure to include it on my ever-changing bucket list. Flash forward to the creation of the *Minimalist Moms Podcast* in autumn of 2016 and the idea became a bit more tangible. I wondered if an opportunity might present itself at some point, but even then, I wasn't willing to start because … well, it just seemed like a daunting endeavor.

Jump to December 1, 2019. I'd been thinking a lot about goal-setting (as we were one month away from a new year) and considered the following questions:

- What would I like to achieve?
- How would I like to change?
- In what ways could I grow?

As I was pondering these things, the thought occurred to me: why wait for the new year? Why do I need a new month or year to pursue change? I can begin to pursue change in the next moment. If I take the opportunity to start today, to just begin, I am one step closer to becoming a better version of myself. I'm taking one step toward those goals I have set before me.

There is no rule that says you must wait until a new year, a new month, or a new day. Just start. You're taking control of your time. You're prioritizing to-dos to make more room for white space—the space that doesn't have to be designated to anything other than what feels best in the moment.

Stop allowing yourself to live passively. Create intention today that aids in the growth of your future self.

What are some goals that you've continued to put off? Maybe financial freedom. Starting a garden. Learning how to play guitar. Your health goals. How about connections you've been meaning to make or relationships you've been meaning to mend? What about ones that involve your children? Why are you continuing to delay? There's no time like the present. Adding more debt, more time, more distance, or more calories between you and your goal will only make the endeavor harder.

What areas do you need to hone? If you're feeling overwhelmed by all that you'd like to pursue, narrow your focus. What professional, financial, social, or physical goals will you set today? How about family or spiritual goals? As you narrow your focus on these smaller goals, you'll see that starting today is easier than you thought. Baby steps. That will aid in momentum.

"We aren't guaranteed tomorrow." "Your future self will thank you." You've heard these cliché statements before, but have you ever really pondered them? How will you feel tomorrow when you've yet to accomplish those things you promised yourself? Starting today puts the ball back in your court. You're the commander of your days.

Why continue to put off that mental to-do (or desire) list? Unaccomplished goals lead to mental clutter. They keep nagging at you and add stress or guilt to your days. Declutter them from your life. Start today.

 MINIMALIST MOM ACTION STEP: What is something you've been putting off in the hopes of starting tomorrow or the next day? Instead of prolonging the decision, act! This mindset has been quite freeing to me whenever I "slip" while pursuing my goals. I can always restart—I can even start today!

I'd love to see what goals you've decided to start today! Use the hashtag #minimalistmoms on Instagram to share with our community.

HABIT STACK

Let me fill you in on a little secret. (Okay, okay, it may not be so much of a secret since I learned about it through other minimalists.) It's the idea of habit stacking. As the name suggests, this means simply stacking one habit onto another that you already have implemented.

I've found habit stacking to be beneficial for building new habits into my existing routine. If I already practice one behavior, why not attach another to it? The connectivity makes all the difference in maintaining new habits you'd like to develop.

Let me give you an example from my own life. I've long wanted to cultivate the habit of nightly pushups. So I asked myself, what's something I do each night before I go to bed? Brush my teeth, of course! So to incorporate this new habit, after I put my toothbrush back in the cabinet, I drop to the ground and do ten or so pushups. It's been easy to cultivate this habit because I've attached it to something I already do each night. Brushing my teeth is a no-brainer, so attaching to it something else I desire to do makes the new task also part of my routine.

Author Norman Vincent Peale discusses the importance of repetition, saying:

> *"Repetition of the same thought or physical action develops into a habit which, repeated frequently enough, becomes an automatic reflex."*

An automatic reflex. Reflexes are involuntary and typically happen instantaneously in response to stimulus. Can you get yourself to a point where the habits you desire to cultivate become reflexive? Think back on your life and see when this has happened before. I'm sure there are more examples than you initially think.

You are likely also familiar with the phrase "'We are what we repeatedly do." If this is the case (which I believe it is), then habit stacking is our most foolproof way to succeed in cementing new habits we desire for ourselves.

Minimalism is a habit you can stack onto your routine. For example, if you do the dishes once a day, stack the habit of a ten-minute declutter on top of it. Take advantage of the strong mental connections you already make each day and habit stack!

 <u>MINIMALIST MOM ACTION STEP:</u> Consider one of your positive habits. Now, name another habit you'd like to cultivate. Can you pair the two of these together? If not, which habits in your life would make sense working with one another?

STOP SCROLLING, START SEIZING

For some reason, I can't read the name of this focus area without thinking of the lyrics to the song from the musical, *Newsies*: "Open the gates and seize the day. Don't be afraid and don't delay...Arise and seize the day!" Are you familiar with this?

Moving on...

Let's backtrack a bit to the idea I want to discuss: the notorious scroll. You open up social media to see who has recently liked or commented on your photo. You're elated. Now it's time to see what others have been up to. You refresh your feed, a new photo pops up, and the scrolling begins. You double tap the screen for someone's new puppy, fresh flowers from the farmers market, a steaming mug of coffee, the introduction of a business venture, toes in the sand at a beach somewhere on the Outer Banks islands...

Before you know it, thirty minutes (or often more) have passed without you pausing to look up. For those thirty minutes, you were living your life by watching others live theirs.

How often does this scrolling habit burden you? Instead of paying the "scroll toll" (as my husband likes to call it), how about you stop scrolling and start seizing?

I'm not advocating for a complete dissolution of your social media accounts, but I am suggesting an overhaul. Cal Newport, author of the book *Digital Minimalism*, asks, "What happens when you are constantly escaping life through a screen?" How would you answer this?

Have you ever considered that you're escaping your life when you scroll for hours throughout your day?

I'll be honest and admit that I've struggled with this—still do! My phone is a distraction from motherhood. Since I don't have as many notable distractions these days, picking up my phone is a mini-vacation when I'm feeling stressed or overwhelmed. Embarrassing, but true. It's easy to become fixated by the pull our phones have over us, but if we're truly honest with ourselves, what do we gain by giving in to it?

Put down your phone, and pick up your life.

We're living our lives through others' experiences on social media instead of creating our own. You could be out there booking a trip, strolling through a farmers market, chatting over coffee with friends, starting a blog. I've said it before: stop waiting and just begin. Stop scrolling, stop with the excuses, and seize opportunities that you've said "no" to because you were too distracted.

As minimalist moms, we not only need to clear out the physical things that weigh us down, but mental ones too.

Declutter the scrolling habit from your days and you will gain back time you never realized you had.

There is life to be away from of your device. Carpe diem. Stop scrolling, start seizing.

 MINIMALIST MOM ACTION STEP: There are a couple of things you could do to start seizing more opportunities in your life. One critical action is to set boundaries on your screen time. Apple products have the ability to set limits on social media, which has helped me immensely in the past. Secondly, rediscover hobbies and behaviors you enjoy and find meaningful. They don't have to be extravagant. Anything to get you to start seizing your life will do.

JUST ONE MINUTE

As a mother of three, I'm constantly looking for ways to streamline decisions and make life run more smoothly. Simple and efficient is the name of the game. If I'm not on top of clutter and mess, I find that I spend too much time addressing them at the end of my days, when what I'm really ready for is bed. After various productivity trials and errors over the years, I've found something that works wonders. It's actually a tip I first learned from author Gretchen Rubin called "The One-Minute Rule."

Clothes need to be put in the hamper. That coat needs to be hung up in the closet. The latest mail needs to be sorted. Plates from lunch need to get washed. You'd be surprised by how much you could accomplish each day just by implementing something as simple as this rule—and you just need one minute.

Consistently taking just one minute to answer an email, file a paper, replenish the diaper supply, or complete whatever other small task needs your attention, saves time and energy that you may not have at the end of your day (or at an otherwise inconvenient time). By taking charge of the small things throughout your day, you'll notice how you have more time and energy to focus on the bigger things.

Rubin herself explains it this way:

> *"Because the tasks are so quick, it isn't too hard to make myself follow the rule— but it has big results. Keeping all those small, nagging tasks under control makes me more serene, less overwhelmed."*

Taking one minute now sneaks in productivity and saves you from a late-night list of to-dos.

Ultimately, I end up saving myself time in the evening by completing tasks throughout my day. I don't want to put my children to bed only to come out to a home that needs thirty minutes or more to be put "back together." Those little things can be done throughout my day (and without much of a burden in the moment). Why not just get them done? They take just one minute.

MINIMALIST MOM ACTION STEP: Consider your end-of-day responsibilities. Write them down (this helps me to actually see what needs to be accomplished and what's essential). Go through the list and see what you could accomplish in just one minute throughout your day instead of stockpiling it for the end. Dishes, hanging up clothes, sorting the mail—whatever it may be, could doing it earlier benefit you?

QUIT TO WIN

"Quitters never prosper." Have you ever heard this quote? Well, I'd like to challenge that notion.

In some regards, yes, the phrase is true. For example, if you're a high school athlete (or really any athlete) on the pursuit of excellence then, well, it's probably best if you don't quit. Keep at it. But sometimes going hard results in injury. Sometimes going hard results in missing your child's ballet recital. Sometimes going hard results in losing relationships due to lack of nurturing. I'm not knocking the quote, but it's important to remember that not all advice will be to our benefit in every situation.

What if instead of overloading yourself, you quit the things standing in the way of what ultimately makes you "win"? This goes against a culture that glorifies being busy and achieving success, but your life and your "wins" are worth taking a stand for.

Our children need to see us follow through on our commitments. On the other hand, if we're failing at home because we're overcommitted elsewhere, well, we must quit to win! Don't enter into these decisions with fear; rather, enter with confidence knowing that you're doing something that will be to your benefit. Your children will notice your new availability. Create space for them, too, as it factors into their creativity and growth. A lot of kids try to fill up their lives in order to get into the perfect school, but they could benefit from being really great at *one* thing. In an effort to be well-rounded, sometimes it's good to cut things out so we can focus our energy on something we really value.

It's important to find something you love that you can work hard at, but when you're "losing" at life, you need to re-evaluate. I'm not advocating for you to quit something for no reason. This isn't a sign to back out of commitments. I'm simply recommending the importance of noting and addressing areas that are holding you back.

When you begin anything— a project, job, any commitment— it's important to set an end date. Don't allow your commitments to remain open-ended. Commit for a season and re-evaluate. In the end, if you decide that it's time to quit, you'll have already set that boundary.

 MINIMALIST MOM ACTION STEP: What areas in your life could benefit from quitting in order to win? Are you working too hard? Spreading yourself too thin with volunteer opportunities? Whenever you say "no" to something, you're saying "yes" to something else.

UNFRIEND, UNSUBSCRIBE, UNFOLLOW

We're living in a remarkable age of technology, friends. I know I don't have to tell you that—the little device in your pocket is evidence enough that you already know the capability you currently possess. You have the ability to cultivate friendships halfway across the world via email and social media. You can access your favorite store's entire catalog from your couch, with the latest outfit delivered to your door in two days or less. You can view photos of what your friend in France ate for breakfast that morning. You're aware that your high school friend is currently vacationing in Bali. You're able to witness the physical transformation of a fitness journey, or the heartbreaking trajectory of a stranger's cancer diagnosis.

No matter how you're connecting, it'd be foolish to ignore the numerous benefits to our connectivity these days. But as Uncle Ben says in *Spider-Man*, "With great power, comes great responsibility." That's why this mantra is: unfriend, unsubscribe, unfollow.

Why are you following people that make you feel "less than," or make you fall into the comparison trap? I'm met with sighs anytime I recommend the idea of unfollowing to others. Please remember: we're usually interacting with carefully constructed profiles, not genuine friends. Consider keeping those that build you up, inform, or entertain you, and unfollow the rest. With a couple of clicks, you can banish those negative emotions you presently feel.

Have you tried implementing this suggestion? If not, what's stopping you?

It can be a challenge to navigate the "unfriend" element of this task, but you have to ask yourself: why do you really follow this person? Why do you allow them to take up precious headspace? There are too many emotions we regularly juggle, so why allow the latest influencer to live in your brain rent-free?

You may be asking what all this has to do with minimalism. Spend your time on someone or something that adds value to your life. Don't add to your mental clutter. Unfriend. Unsubscribe. Unfollow.

 MINIMALIST MOM ACTION STEP: This action step is straightforward: sort through the individuals you're following and click "unfollow" on those that don't positively serve you.

Your mental health is too important to give time away to those who make you feel inferior!

REDUCE YOUR CHOICES

I'm sure that by this point, you're familiar with the term "decision fatigue." For those of you who aren't, let me fill you in on how it works. Every day, we're faced with hundreds of decisions to make. As morning turns to afternoon, and afternoon turns to night, our ability to make the best decisions wanes.

Consider all of the choices you must make each morning:

- What will I wear?
- What should I have for breakfast?
- What should my children have for breakfast?
- Where are my keys?
- Does my child have everything they need for school?
- How will I best navigate this traffic jam?

...and this is all before you get to work or drop your children off at school.

When you apply the mentality of choice reduction, you streamline the decision-making process.

There are so many decisions throughout your day that you can make routine. For example, I feed my children the same thing for breakfast each morning. We'll usually switch it up every couple of months, but day after day, we have oatmeal with milk, butter, and a sprinkle of brown sugar. Luckily, my kids don't seem to mind. I don't have to think about it, and it's easy to prep. I'm reducing the number of choices I have to make, and avoiding having to consider other factors, such as whether or not my children will eat it or if there will be enough to go around. I know this wouldn't work for everyone, so if that's your case, maybe limit it to two or three easy-to-prep breakfasts that everyone enjoys.

Consider your to-do list: reducing your choices creates space to focus on the tasks you've deemed important enough to remain on the list. When you reduce the choices you have to

Sometimes when we focus on the loss rather than the gain, we lose sight of the big picture goal and dwell on what we perceive as loss in the present moment. Whenever you say "no" to one thing, you say "yes" to another, and vice versa. Instead of looking at the things you hope not to miss, why not focus on that which you gain?

When applied to minimalism, you can see that as you set the priority to own less stuff, you are choosing more of something else. You are conserving your time, money, and physical space. Who wouldn't be more joyful about that? Choose JOMO.

 MINIMALIST MOM ACTION STEP: Set boundaries with your phone. Don't look at it after a certain hour in the evening, or first thing in the morning. Better yet, take a screen-free week! Don't measure your experiences by the way others are living theirs. Remember JOMO as you set your phone down and seek out the joy around you!

PUT IT DOWN

These days, you hear about how important it is to put your phone down and connect to those around you:

"Stop scrolling, put it down!"

"I'm sitting right in front of you. Put it down!"

Area of Focus: Time Minimalism

"Do you really need to take your phone to the bathroom? Put it down!" (Yes, I went there.)

We hear the words "put it down" when it comes to our phones—something tangible—but what about things in life that are harder to notice? What else should you "put down" in this season? Maybe it's the book club you've been a member of since its inception that's no longer serving a purpose. Maybe it's the weight of a family member's burdens. Maybe it's your responsibility to the school PTA that takes up too much time in your schedule.

Putting things down ultimately depends on boundaries. Don't let people pleasing or mindlessness keep you tied to the unnecessary load. Put down the things that carry over into your mind, emotions, and relationships—especially your relationships with your children.

I once heard a quote that said, "Showing strength is also knowing when to put down the weight and rest." What is weighing on you these days? Put it down.

 MINIMALIST MOM ACTION STEP: How will you benefit from "putting down" responsibilities, tasks, or roles in your life? Will you have more free time, increased productivity (towards the things you actually want to do), personal growth, or better sleep? Take action and reap the reward.

LET'S SIMPLIFY:
PREGNANCY &
POSTPARTUM
MINIMALISM

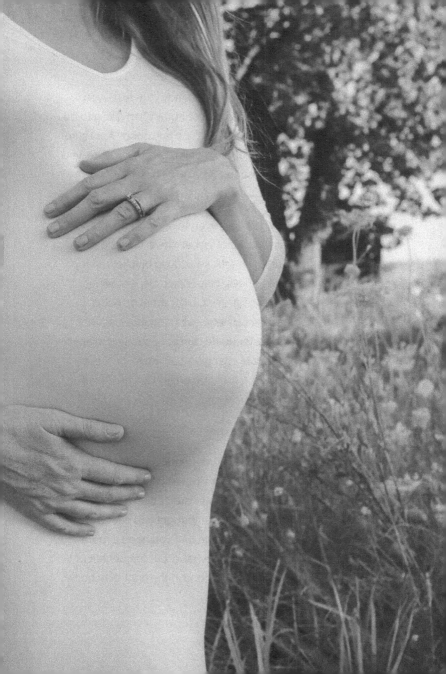

MOTHERHOOD

It's official, there are two lines on that handy little test—you're pregnant. A rush of thoughts floods your brain: "I'm going to be a mother. Wait, how do I do that? Will I be any good? Am I sure it's the right time? How will I afford a child?" And, of course, you eventually land on the question, "What will I need?"

If you do a quick Google search for "baby registry," you'll come upon list after list detailing everything you'll need: crib, diaper changing station, washcloths, bath toys, faucet cover, waterproof mattress, fitted sheets, swaddling blankets, sleep sacks, hats, bathing suits, shoes, diaper pail, diapers, wipes, wipe warmer, rocking chair, bassinet, baby monitor, noise machine, baby books, bins, baskets, swing, bouncer, activity mat, blocks, books, lovies, teethers, car seats, strollers, diaper bags, changing pad, *portable* changing pad, travel crib, baby carrier, stroller bunting bag…I could go on and on, but I think you get the picture.

My question for you is: what is essential?

The definition of essential will shift depending on who you come into contact with. Plenty of well-meaning parents will mention things you never knew existed ("pee-pee teepees" and "nose fridas"), let alone thought you needed. It's countercultural to challenge the idea that you need a room full of possessions for your newborn babe, but the benefit of doing so will set you up for motherhood in the right direction.

I typically wouldn't take such a strong stance, but I strongly protest to overconsumption in early motherhood. The literal weight of carrying a thirty-pound diaper bag is unnecessary. Shed the excess.

The problem with baby gear is that it's useful, but temporary. There are various purchases you'll need to make when pregnant, but you should consider the areas in which you can simplify.

The other thing is this: stores will remain available to you post-baby arrival. If at some point during those initial weeks you realize that you've forgotten something, don't worry. You can always run out and grab what you need, or ask about it in your friend network. The advantage to this approach is that it stops you from cluttering your home as you prepare for your new arrival. You're keeping only what you've deemed essential and are preventing items that you'll never actually use from taking up space. Buy things when you reach a need milestone, not before!

When it comes to the creation of the baby registry, I suggest doing it in a couple of segments. My personal process was as follows: arrive at the baby store, open the registry, and scan the items. We made sure to scan as many items we thought we'd want (multiple strollers, car seats, wraps, etc.). Don't limit yourself at this point. Where our process varied from a standard experience is that we didn't spend time in the store comparing which items were "better." Every item we

Let's Simplify: Pregnancy & Postpartum Minimalism

scanned provided details and customer ratings, and this felt overwhelming to me. I didn't want to make the wrong decision as we were compiling our list, so instead of taking hours to configure the exact items we wanted, we saved that process for later. While at home (at my leisure) I was able to go through the items and compare which ones I preferred. I narrowed things down on my own time (over a week or so) and then had a solid list of high-quality, positively-reviewed baby items. In a desire to eliminate as much stress as possible from the registration process, scanning as many items in store and then whittling down the list at home just made sense.

As you craft your list, call to mind the necessities: what items will you use for longer than a couple of months? Invest in

those things. Some examples from my life were the pack 'n play, baby carrier, and stroller.

THE ESSENTIALS

- **Diapers**: It's up to you whether or not you want to use cloth diapers. There are benefits to both disposable and cloth. This topic is a little too complicated to dive into here, but I included it in this section for obvious reasons.

- **A place to sleep**:

  - Mattress
  - Crib Sheets (2–3). It's nice to have more than one in case there's a potty accident in the middle of the night.
  - Mattress cover (2). Again, it's nice to have more than one in case of a potty accident.

- **Clothing**: Don't go overboard in this area. I'd also suggest registering for baby clothes in various stages throughout that first year. I only had a handful of newborn items. All three of my babies ended up in newborn clothes for only one week.

- **Blankets**: I suggest 3–4 blankets in which you're able to swaddle your baby. Muslin blankets are breathable and can be used even in the summer months.

- **Bath soap**

- **Car seat**: I recommend finding a car seat with a corresponding stroller frame. We did this for our third, and I wish we would've done it for the first two. The stroller frame itself was fairly inexpensive, and it beats having to lug around a heavy car seat everywhere you go. Don't make it harder than it needs to be at this stage. Also, this is definitely something you could resell on Facebook Marketplace when you're finished with it.

NICE TO HAVE

- **A place to rest:** While you don't need a million gadgets, it is nice to have a contained space (e.g., swing, bouncer, mat, pack 'n play) that you can utilize when cooking dinner or taking a shower. If the swing is small

enough, you can easily tote it into the bathroom with you to keep an eye on your little one while you shower. You can typically use a swing for five or six months and then store it for your next baby or donate/sell it to someone else.

- **Bottles:** This truly depends on the baby and whether or not you plan to nurse. If you're a working mother, you may want five or six on hand, but I think most could get by with two or three. That said, I didn't end up using a bottle with two of my three children. My boys didn't seem to care for the bottle, and because it wasn't a necessity, I ended up taking all of my daughter's bottles and donating them to a local mothers' center.

- **Bookbag /diaper bag:** Don't call me crazy quite yet, I'm only suggesting that you could use a backpack *instead* of a diaper bag to carry around your baby's necessities. I've honestly been able to manage carrying a large handbag with a couple of diapers, wipes, a binkie, and muslin blanket. To tote around a bag full of items "just in case" has never sounded ideal for me. If you'd like to have an extra outfit, heavier blanket, or whatever you deem necessary close by, I recommend keeping a small basket of these items in your trunk. That way, if you really find yourself in a bind, you can just run to your vehicle instead of toting the items around with you.

Let's Simplify: Pregnancy & Postpartum Minimalism

TAKE IT OR LEAVE IT (OPTIONAL)

- **Burp cloth**
- **Changing station**
- **Nursing pillow**
- **Nursing cover:** I used a cover with my first child. My second, however, was born in mid-July. We were outside not long after he was born, and I remember looking down at him (under the cover) and thinking of how hot he must have been under there. It was then and there that I took off the cover and never looked back. You can most definitely nurse your baby without a cover, and do not allow anyone to make you feel ashamed for doing so. This comfort level will vary for the individual, and there may be certain circumstances in which you'd want more coverage. For those moments, I just use the muslin blanket to cover myself.

ITEMS TO INVEST IN

- **Stroller**: One of the items I almost always suggest investing in is a nice stroller.
- **Monitor**: I highly recommend investing in a quality baby monitor, preferably one with a camera. That said, I don't think your monitor needs all the bells and whistles. (I will say that the microphone on my side was really nice to have when my toddler was misbehaving.)

- **Highchair**: You'll need a highchair once your baby begins to sit up and spoon feed. When I say "invest" in a quality chair, I don't necessarily mean spend a ton of money (I have a $20 basic chair from Ikea). I *do* mean you'll need to buy one. I love the option of having a basic chair, but there are also slightly pricier chairs that can be adjusted as your child grows.

- **Wrap**: If you're an individual who plans to wear your baby, make sure to invest in a high-quality wrap. This is especially helpful as you add more than one child. You're able to have two hands free while keeping your baby safe on your chest.

- **Hand pump**: To the best of my knowledge, some insurance companies provide new mothers with electronic pumps. I used one with my first baby.

However, after having more than one child, I found it much easier to just use a hand pump. I was able to express milk much quicker and didn't have to get all "hooked up." I also loved the hand pump for on-to-go needs. It fit well in my handbag, and I was able to pump and dump easily in public.

- **Pack 'n Play**: This is another one of those items that proves to be even more useful as you add children. It's also great for your child, as it alleviates the need for a bassinet when you have a newborn. A quality pack 'n play can be used as a portable crib and safe play area for years to come (or like I said, when you have more than one and want a safe area to contain them when dealing with your other children). We use ours every day, and my children have all taken it for sleepovers with their grandparents.

A COUPLE OF ITEMS I DON'T UNDERSTAND

- **Wipe warmers**: I get it, you want your baby to feel comfortable during those late-night changes. However, babies have been cleaned/wiped for thousands of years, and this just seems quite unnecessary. I'd most definitely skip this item, especially if you're looking for ways to save money.

- **Baby food makers**: A great way to save money is to make your own baby food, and you can easily use your own blender or food processor. I'd steer clear of bringing another appliance into your kitchen that will only take up precious counter or cabinet space.

SOME GREAT WAYS TO SAVE MONEY WHILE PREGNANT AND POSTPARTUM

- **Breastfeeding**: When it comes to feeding your baby, there's nothing cheaper than breast milk. Of course, everyone's circumstances are different with regard to this element of motherhood. I'm not here to condemn your choice either way, but if you're strictly looking to save money, this is the way to go. For those who are able, breastfeeding is a wonderful way to nourish your babies without any extra equipment, sterilizing, or washing up!
- **Breast pumps**: Some insurance companies offer free pumps to mothers.
- **Other ways to save**: Sign up for a baby registry (tell people what you need and remind them that you are trying to stick to a list); share items with friends or family; check buy-nothing groups or Facebook Marketplace; and if you plan on having another baby, store the items for later. I've had friends sell the majority of their baby items only to buy them again after having a second

babe. Seems like a waste of money and time when you can simply store them until you're done having children.

Is there something you'd add to any of these lists? Or maybe something you'd take off? Let me know on Instagram @minimalistmomspodcast!

I want to end this section by saying this: if you've done (or intend to do) something that seems counter to what I've said, that's okay! As with any area of life, there will be various opinions and voices speaking on what we should or shouldn't be doing (I'm one of them—ha!). Condense the voices you're listening to and make the best decision for *you*. Don't put pressure on yourself to be prepared with "all of the things." *You* are the most important thing that your baby needs. Once they arrive, spend time taking care of yourself and your baby. In my experience, people are happy to lend a helping hand, so if you find that you're missing something, ask for help.

I won't say that it's easy to condense this area. It takes deliberate decisions and clear boundaries communicated to those around you. Don't compare the decisions you've made to those of other expectant mothers. Living with less provides you with more time, space, and money—three things you'll be thankful to have as a new mom.

I would never suggest following the health plan of a stranger while you're pregnant. Just because you see another pregnant woman/new mother beginning a new meal plan and doing CrossFit doesn't mean you should 1) compare yourself to what they're doing, or 2) begin such an extreme change from your norm. Give yourself grace and remember that lifestyle choices are relative. The same goes for parenting. While wise counsel has its place, the decisions you make for your child are personal and can only be made by you.

You've done the work of seeking out information, educating yourself, and showing investment in this little one. It is my personal belief that anyone that shows this enthusiasm for motherhood is already a great mother. Continue to navigate through the voices and trust yourself.

MINIMALISM & NEWBORNS: WHAT EVERYDAY MINIMALIST MOMS ARE SAYING

Nikki: Do *not* rush to get tons of baby stuff! I am ready to deliver baby number four and have very carefully acquired what we need from friends. Don't buy into the idea that you need lots of items (especially ones that have a big carbon footprint!).

Becky: Be realistic about what your new baby "needs." Registry prompt lists promote so many items as "essentials" that really aren't.

Judith: This is awfully basic, but I was stressing out at the end of the pregnancy because we didn't have a room ready for the baby (the crib was in our bedroom), and my midwife said, "All the baby needs is you." Not entirely accurate of course, but it is still such a good reminder when everyone is trying to sell you things you supposedly need for a baby! I also recommend picking gender neutral car seats, highchairs, etc., so that you don't feel compelled to buy those big-ticket items again if you have more than one child and they're not the same sex/gender.

Kristen: Only purchase a handful of maternity tops and bottoms in solid colors that you can mix and match. Then accessorize with different scarves, cardigans, sweaters, etc., so it doesn't look like you're wearing the same things over and over! It was very helpful to not load up on clothes I'd only wear for a few months!

Megan: The thing your baby needs most is *you*. Nursing, snuggling, rocking, reading, singing—all of these actions are so much more valuable than the best swaddle, rocker, toy, etc.

Kate: I wasn't into minimalism until I had toddlers, but one of the reasons I got into it was because I found pregnancy and postpartum so difficult. I'm very passionate now, and as a physical therapist working with pregnant women, I always emphasize the importance of postpartum rest. This includes a reduced schedule and reduced mental clutter to allow healing.

Marie: Borrow things from friends, declutter your house before the baby comes, and have a place for everything. Also, babies don't need their own towels.

Let's Simplify: Pregnancy & Postpartum Minimalism

AREA OF FOCUS:
MINDFULNESS

Emotional
and Mental
Decluttering

ONLY FOR A SEASON

I don't know about you, but typically around the conclusion of February, I'm just about done. I'm done with the cold Ohio weather. I'm done being stuck inside. I'm done with any viruses my youngest child may have caught (who, prior to preschool, rarely had a case of the sniffles). I'm ready for spring. I'm ready for some sunshine. I'm ready to be in a new season—both literally and metaphorically.

The funny thing is that prior to motherhood, I *loved* the late fall and winter months. I love giant coats, cozy sweaters, and snow boots. I felt like I was at my best in these months. There's something about dark winter days that allows for self-preservation and rejuvenation. Basically, I could've been a brown bear in another life.

But that all changed when I became a mother. Gone are the days when I could snuggle under a blanket and read a book for hours. Gone are the post-church naps. Sure, I could probably enlist my husband to help out with these things, but the ease with which they'd organically happen is gone...at least for now.

At least for a season.

That's why this area of focus is just that: only for a season.

As mothers we have to remind ourselves that we will have to put some of our own desires on the back burner "only for a season." Only for a season will our kiddos need regular supervision that takes us away from afternoon naps or extended reading time. But on the other hand, we can get to thinking ...

Only for a season will our children allow us to snuggle them in our laps. Only for a season will they need us to wipe their runny noses. Only for a season will we be the only ones to calm them after a skinned knee.

Our babies will be little only for a season. We won't always have to pick up toys from the floor—it's only for a season. We'll soon wish we enjoyed that time more. We'll realize that, despite the short season, we wished it would've lasted a lifetime.

 MINIMALIST MOM ACTION STEP: Today, I want you to take the time to write down ten things you're grateful for, *specifically* in this season of life. Share them with your spouse/partner, another mom, or even your children.

SLOW DOWN

I set out on a walk with my two littles, as I figured it'd be a great way for all of us to release some energy. My thinking was that they'd get tired out before nap time, and I'd have a bit of a workout. Win-win.

Less than eight hundred feet from our back door, we already stopped to check out the wildflowers. "Come on! We're going for a walk," I said. My daughter picked up the pace only to stop again after a couple more minutes of walking. "We don't have time for that! Mommy said this was time to walk, let's go." I picked up my pace a bit in hopes that she'd follow along, and that's when it hit me.

You've done it again, I thought. In an effort to push my agenda, I failed to accept the moment for what it was. What was the hurry? We had nowhere to be and really no schedule. To quote Daniel Tiger, "Sometimes it's good to go slow."

Getting rid of clutter isn't just a tangible endeavor, but an emotional one as well. Clutter in our minds keeps us from slow living. To slow down is to live intentionally and consciously, to prioritize self-care. While I do believe that there's a time for a more fast-paced approach, more often than not, our lives could use a bit of slowing down.

Take a step back and watch your child eat their pancakes. Look on as they build a castle of blocks, or as they flip through books. Remove distractions while you sit with your morning cup of coffee. Put your phone away while your partner shares their day with you. Invest in those around you by slowing down and giving conscious attention.

I've found that I'm a much more relaxed individual when I'm not rushing from moment to moment. When I say "no" more often. When I keep my mind and schedule from becoming overcrowded and overburdened. I need to let my daughter slow down and enjoy the wildflowers, the lawn gnome, the giant rock that she strategically climbs and jumps off.

When we embrace a minimalist approach to life, we give priority to what's important to us—our family, friends, possessions, and hobbies. To slow down is to remain present. And friends, what else is better than living in the present moment? Slow down, you won't regret it.

 MINIMALIST MOM ACTION STEP: In what areas do you struggle to slow down? Do you rush through moments with your children? Take the time to remove distractions and notice. Make this a regular practice.

> I'd love to see how you've chosen to slow down! Use the hashtag #minimalistmoms on Instagram to share your moments with our community.

RECEIVE REST

It doesn't take an investigator to notice the exhausted, deprived individual in today's society. Our culture applauds the relentless pursuit of success and productivity. We value being busy. But at what cost? We might have money in the bank, a nice car, home, and possessions to show for it—but to what detriment? We over-schedule our days, our weeks. We're hurried. We rarely set aside time to stop or renew. We end up losing time with our family, friends, ourselves...Why do we do this?

This area of focus is to remind you to *receive rest*.

When you rest, you refresh your mind and body, you restore your soul. Countless studies suggest how important it is to rest. Author Wayne Muller puts our need for rest this way:

> *"Like a path through the forest, Sabbath [rest] creates a marker for ourselves so, if we are lost, we can find our way back to our center."*

You don't need to take up a daily yoga practice (unless you want to) or lay around your house for twenty-four hours straight to receive rest. Maybe for you, rest looks like a quiet walk through the woods once per week. Maybe it looks like an afternoon without checking your cell phone or work emails. Maybe it looks like a Sunday brunch with friends, or cooking dinner with your family on a Tuesday evening. No interruptions. No distractions. While the method of rest looks different for each of us, I'm a firm believer that all options offer similar benefits.

The aim of this book is to aid you in your pursuit of less in order to receive more. When we regularly set time aside to rest, we strengthen other endeavors. We have the momentum to succeed because we've experienced rejuvenation. We have taken time for ourselves. We have given our minds time to recharge.

I've found that when I neglect rest in my own life, it's evident. I'm irritable, bitter, and I tend to lash out at my husband and children. It is *critical* that I incorporate weekly (if not daily) rest into my schedule. I am far more capable when this is a deliberate priority. As a mother, it can be difficult to figure out when to rest. If I'm not spending time with my children, I'm maintaining my household, doing laundry, dishes, vacuuming—you know the list, you have your own!

How do we squeeze in rest without it feeling hurried or like just another "chore"? Be purposeful. If you need to, put it in your schedule. Discuss rest with your spouse or partner—I'm sure they need it just as much as you. Come together and compromise on how to make it happen. Don't allow another week to go by neglecting this area. Your body, your mind, your children, your spouse/partner—truly everyone will benefit!

Here is your friendly reminder to receive rest.

 MINIMALIST MOM ACTION STEP: Prioritize rest this week. Set a timer for bed and make sure you follow it. Turn off the screens and pick up a book instead. Visualize how you'll feel

Area of Focus: Mindfulness

in the morning when you've given yourself that important self-care.

SEIZE SILENCE

We go about our lives surrounded by so much noise: our families, coworkers, friends, spouses/partners, our busy commutes, and the general noise from being in public. Mothers experience noise on a whole new level. From the moment we rise to the moment we sleep, noise is everywhere.

"Mom! Look at this!"
"Mom, can you get me [insert item]."
"Mom, they hit me!"
"Mom, did you know...[insert obscure or new-to-them fact]?"

Children are *loud*. This is the new soundtrack of our lives. It's not a particularly bad thing, but combining the external and internal noise leaves us with very little time to experience silence that isn't intentionally planned. By the end of the day, the "noise" seems impossible to escape.

In *Digital Minimalism*, Cal Newport writes:

> "...when you avoid solitude, you miss out on the positive things it brings you: the ability to clarify hard problems, to regulate your emotions, to build moral courage, and

to strengthen relationships. If you suffer from chronic solitude deprivation, therefore, the quality of your life degrades."

When we avoid solitude or silence, there are negative repercussions. We're more irritable towards our children. We lack patience. I've even experienced headaches from noise overwhelm. But we shouldn't be surprised. We need to act in order to combat this problem. We must seize solitude, silence.

How can you incorporate more silence into your day? I'm talking no music, no podcasts, no audiobooks. Silence. Maybe you'll find walking in silence to be beneficial. Maybe it's sipping a cup of coffee or tea on your couch. Maybe it's making your commute a silent ride.

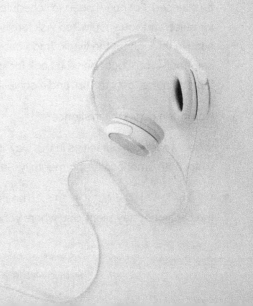

I've struggled doing this myself. I absolutely love having a podcast going while I cook, wash the dishes, fold the laundry, or drive. But see, then there's no room for me to just "be" with my thoughts. The constant noise in my head doesn't seem exhausting, but when I step back and get perspective, it's a contributor to the noise.

I decided to practice this before I encouraged you all to do so. I took my son to the doctor the other day and as I sat in the waiting room, I didn't pick up my cell phone. I didn't read a magazine. I just sat in silence. It was difficult at first—the habit is to reach down and scroll through my phone. It felt odd to just sit, but I did it.

I'd like to think that I'll have more opportunities for silence as my children grow older and I have more alone time. However, there will always be some kind of noise needing to be silenced. For now, I need to schedule in times of my day for quiet, and you should, too. Ask family members to help pitch in throughout the week. Trade babysitting times with a neighbor—you'll both benefit! Look for specific times of day that the noise "gets to you" and resolve it!

How often do you sit in silence?

When we refresh ourselves in this way, it is so beneficial to our state, both emotionally and mentally. Seize silence.

 MINIMALIST MOM ACTION STEP: The next time you're in the car alone, stay silent. See where your thoughts take you.

Consider taking a walk after dinner or when the kids are in bed. Listen to the birds settling down. What do you notice that you otherwise wouldn't have if you rushed through the moment?

You Do You

When it comes to minimalism, one of the sentences I tend to say the most is: minimalism looks different for everyone. I've said it on the podcast, during interviews, and to friends and family. There's an idea that minimalism is stripping your home of all color and character. This misconception is one of only white walls and functional furniture for the members of the household, where all but a handful of toys for your children are whittled away. Everything for a reason. Everything has a place.

While I do believe minimalists should move toward that which is essential, I also believe that minimalism is very much a tool you should utilize to craft a life specifically geared toward you and your family.

Your minimalist pursuit will not look like mine, and mine will not look like yours. We are each on our own journey. There is no one tracking your progress or setting definite boundaries. That's for you to decide. You do you.

Don't compare your household to those of fellow minimalists. The worst thing you can do is feel forced into making decisions you can't sustainably live with in your day-to-day. If you're making yourself miserable for the sake of "being minimalist," you're doing it wrong. Minimalism is supposed to help, not hinder, the life you desire.

Think about minimalism in this way: define what physical belongings are essential and allow that process to carry over into your mindset. You get to curate your home and set boundaries on your schedule. You get to select which hobbies you invest time and money into.

Let's say, for example, that you love to scrapbook. This hobby brings you enjoyment, pleasure, and a sense of accomplishment. You have carved out a space in your home where you regularly enjoy this interest. Why would you pare down this area? Yes, maybe you organize your supplies and are intentional about how much you're purchasing, but don't limit yourself for the sake of minimalism. Allow yourself to have the boxes of stickers, the bins of paper, the tools, the glues, the stack of completed books.

Don't spend time stressing about what you do or don't choose to minimize. The fact of the matter is that you're working toward a lifestyle of less. Continue to rid your life of excess and make room for the items you *want* to fit.

I'm practicing minimalism my way, you'll practice it your way. You do you.

 MINIMALIST MOM ACTION STEP: Determine the priorities that bring you *furthest* from the minimalist lifestyle. For my husband, this would be his fascination with camping. He will always own equipment needed for a weekend camping trip. It's stored in a couple of bins in our basement. Look at the hobbies and interests that take up the most space in your home, see if there is any overlap or anything that can be cut. (My husband and his sister share a kayak. It's a minimalist step for him to own fewer things in our house while still contributing to an area that isn't overly minimal.)

TAKE A WALK

One of the simplest (and I'd be willing to say, the most minimalist) ways to improve your mental and physical health would be to get outside. Do you ever notice how stepping outside is an automatic mood booster? Even in the winter, I'll step out onto my front stoop, take a deep breath, and instantly feel a little bit better. The fresh air is beneficial—it clears our heads, and often, is a simple way to reset what has been broken or highlight what is in need of fixing.

One of the defining characteristics of a minimalist is keenness on finding the simplest path to reaching a particular goal. When it comes to self-care, there is probably no easier habit to adopt than walking. It's innate. Whether we're walking, jogging, or running, it's the simplest way to get from here to there (even if "there" is just a mental space we need to return to). It doesn't matter if it's for ten minutes or a couple of hours, the action of unplugging and stripping away distractions is highly beneficial.

What about walking to combat conflict? Whether we're navigating a toddler tantrum or breaking up disputes between siblings, mothers are used to family skirmishes. Have you ever considered that taking a walk could be the answer to the problem? When we set out on a walk, our children are focused on keeping one foot in front of the other. You could even make it a game and set a goal or intention for your time.

Strip down the ideas you've built around health and fitness needing to spend hours in a gym each week. I'm no doctor, but a quick Google search will provide plenty of information on how favorable walking is for your mind and body. Our bodies were *designed* to do this. Stressed at work? Take a thirty-minute walk at lunch to enable focus for the rest of your day. Arguing with your spouse or partner? Take ten minutes to "reboot" and come back to the conversation more rational and less reactive.

Getting outside on a walk breaks us away from our everyday routine. I've noticed that regardless of the weather, my kids are always willing to get out there. It gives us an opportunity to reset and create connection. The ability to take a walk has had a huge impact in my life. I've included it in my evening routine, no matter the weather. You can walk at home, in the woods, on the beach, in the city. There is nothing more simple.

 MINIMALIST MOM ACTION STEP: The next time your children are arguing with one another, take them outside for a walk. See how it affects the mood. Check out the book *In Praise of*

Walking: The New Science of How We Walk and Why It's Good for Us by Shane O'Mara.

KNOW YOURSELF

It's easy to know who you are, right? You know what fulfills you, what makes you happy, what makes you tick, what makes you crazy. You're with yourself twenty-four seven. No one else should know you better than *you*, and yet, moments can arise that make it difficult to differentiate yourself from a stranger.

In the past, I've found that talking with friends and family can help work through these moments, but there are other ways, too. Recently, I stumbled upon a personality test called the Enneagram. Ever heard of it? I'll admit I was a little late to the craze. However, I have found it to be quite insightful when assessing elements of my personality. It provided me with a perspective that I hadn't been able to articulate, and allowed me to think big picture when it came to my life. I've been able to better define my role as wife, mother, friend, and employee. It's truly been an asset.

With that said, though personality tests are helpful, what if we looked at the simplifying of our lives as another type of test? Stay with me here. As you begin to declutter and simplify your home, reflect on the decisions you're making. Those decisions can lead to insights on who you are, what you hold dear, and how you make decisions. Really!

For example, maybe you're struggling to get rid of appliances because you love spending time in the kitchen. This is a space in your home where you create, cook with your children, and relax with a glass of wine or hot cup of coffee. You've chosen to make your kitchen an inviting space filled with the proper tools to be prepared for whatever the recipe may call for. On the other hand, you may struggle to dress yourself each day and have found it much easier to save time and energy by living with less in your closet. Your capsule wardrobe makes it easy for you to make decisions in the morning, and in turn, you're ready to start your day with one less stressful decision to be made.

The process of decluttering your home will include decisions both big and small. As you make these decisions, you will gain confidence in making choices outside of your home that affect not only you, but the people around you! As you simplify, you are *literally* deciding how to surround yourself day-to-day. What could be more insightful to your personality than that?

The examples given above may not seem like a window into one's personality. However, this week, I challenge you to know yourself! Allow time for reflection as you clean out an overwhelmed area of your home. What did you keep? What did you purge? The answers may say more about you than you expected.

 __MINIMALIST MOM ACTION STEP:__ Make a list of the things you've decided to keep and purge. Is there a common theme?

Area of Focus: Mindfulness

Maybe you've purged the older and kept the newer? Maybe you've purged more color and kept neutrals? Whatever your theme may be, continue to use it as you declutter your space

CONTENTMENT OVER COVET

In the fall of 2020, my husband, children, and I finally moved into our "family home." We planned this for nearly eight years of marriage, and at last, it happened. We have a yard. We have a room for our two oldest children. We have a kitchen that's more than five square feet. We have a pantry. We have room for our dog to roam and run. Yes, we finally saw our hard work pay off.

One evening, I was driving to meet a friend in a neighborhood ten minutes away from our new home. In order to get there, I decided to avoid the highway and cut through a more "upscale" neighborhood to the south. The Tudor homes were beautifully architected from stone. As I drove through the tree-lined streets with the sun shining through the autumn leaves, illuminating them ever so beautifully, I began to really look around. Something in me started to rise. I felt...jealous. I felt myself yearning to live there. *How can I make it happen?* I wondered. Mere moments later, it occurred to me: You have a home. You have a yard. You have room for your two oldest children. You have a kitchen that's more than five square feet. You have a pantry. You have room for the dog to roam.

I allowed my mind to drift into coveting that which my neighbor possessed. I allowed my contentment to fade and envy to slip in. And you know what? It was a horrible feeling.

That's why this area of focus is: content over covet.

When we find contentment, it's much harder to desire that which we don't have. To covet is to eagerly seek (or wish for) something. What was I wishing for that I didn't already have?

I had to grab hold of my thoughts. Only through intentionality could I switch my focus. My thoughts were starting down a path of negativity, so I began to meditate on gratitude. Mere moments prior I was feeling content, even privileged, with my new home. Nothing tangible had shifted. It was my mind. When my mind focused on contentment over covetousness, life was much more enjoyable, even peaceful.

Even now, as I look back and reflect on that moment, I get embarrassed. People in this country (and around the world) live with very little, and there I was yearning for *more* because what I had wasn't "new and shiny" anymore. That's the problem with living in the state of "never enough": when you're focused on obtaining more and more, you're left unsatisfied. Despite how wealthy you may be, you will never get to the point of "having it all." Homing your focus in on gratitude will remind you not to "covet" the things you don't have. When we focus on what we do have, we're left fulfilled, satisfied, and content.

<u>MINIMALIST MOM ACTION STEP:</u> Can you pinpoint an area where you've recently felt less than satisfied? Combat your discontented spirit with truths regarding why you already have more than enough in that area. Gratitude lists are a great place to start. Try writing a list of one hundred things you're grateful for—even something as simple as hovering over your kitchen sink, mug of coffee in hand as a cool breeze slips through your window. I recommend the book *The Little Book of Lykke: The Danish Search for the World's Happiest People* by Meik Wiking for a study on six factors that explain happiness across the world. A great children's book on gratitude is *The Perfect Sofa* by Fifi Kuo.

GO TO BED

According to the National Sleep Foundation, sleep is a crucial indicator of our health and well-being, and the average adult should receive seven to nine hours each night. That said, at least 35 percent of American adults that say they log less than seven hours each night. I seldom hear of the benefits of sleep in the minimalist community. However, sleep can be a powerful ally when crafting an intentional life.

I wouldn't say that I've always lived in a way that prioritized sleep. Actually, my life has looked like quite the contrary (especially in the season of having small children). But I'd be lying if I said that it was always the "fault" of a hungry baby or scared-of-the-dark child. More often the "fault" is of my own doing. Let me paint a picture you can maybe relate to: my children are nicely tucked away in their rooms, the couch looks cozy, and the latest episode of *The Bachelor* is calling my name. Before I know it, two hours have passed, I've eaten a bag of popcorn, and I'm no better off than when I began.

What I really should've done was gone to bed. Don't tell me I'm alone here.

It's ironic to me that we value supplements, healthy food, or the latest diet, but we don't do one of the easiest, best things for our health—get a good night's sleep. You've probably said it numerous times to your kids: go to bed! You've probably even been envious of your toddler's mid-day naptime. *Oh! How I wish I were in your shoes, little one. If only I, too, could lay my head on a pillow at 1 p.m. each day.* If I'm regularly envious

of my child's ability to get rest, it's worth considering what's getting in the way of my slumber.

According to the Division of Sleep Medicine at Harvard Medical School, the benefits from a well-rested night are abundant: "[S]leep plays a critical role in immune function, metabolism, memory, learning, and other vital functions." I appreciate the use of the word "vital" when describing the role of sleep. Vital functions of our body are positively or negatively affected by our intentionality. How am I to live an intentional, mindful life if I'm struggling to prioritize my sleep?

As I said, I can trace the lack of sleep back to vegging out for a little too long on the couch. I should also note that sometimes, I'll just be lying in bed paying the "scroll toll" instead of putting my phone down for the night.

Again, I can't say that this has always been an area of strength for me, but I can say that I've paid the price for neglect. My children need me to function at my best and, while sometimes it may not fully be in my control, I can take intentional steps to elevate this area of my life. So whether you need to flip off the television, put down the cell phone, or close the laptop, make sure you are doing so!

Whatever is keeping you from sleep, I'd ask you to fight against it. Declutter it from your days. Go to bed—you'll be thankful you did tomorrow morning.

Set a bedtime alarm on your phone and stick to it! Do this every day for a week and see how you feel. For further information on the benefits of sleep, check out *Why We Sleep* by Matthew Walker, *The Sleep Solution: Why Your Sleep Is Broken and How to Fix It* by W. Chris Winters, and *Sleeping Through the Night: How Infants, Toddlers, and Their Parents Can Get a Good Night's Sleep* by Jodi A. Mindell.

KEEP SMALL THINGS SMALL

There are many lessons I've learned in parenthood, but one that sticks out is knowing when to choose my battles. After failing to see this early on, I now realize that I don't have to engage my children's every potentially problematic behavior.

Is your son lingering near the giant mud puddle out back? You could choose to combat his innate nature to dive headfirst into the puddle, or you could just go with it (despite having to spend some time hosing him down afterwards).

What about the notorious use of the words "butt" and "poop" (i.e., "butt head," "poop face")? I'm sure a lot of you can relate to the frustration felt when a child slings these "potty words" around while cackling at their usage. I'll still request that the words to stop, but it's not the time for me to dig my heels in and yell out consequences (unless they're being slung at the wrong person). In the grand scheme of things, this isn't a "hill to die on," you know?

When I find myself getting frustrated by inconsequential behaviors, I have to remind myself to keep small things small.

If you're like most people, you'll no doubt encounter situations that drain your patience and ability to stay even-tempered. I'd like to suggest that you recognize many of these situations as small things. Oftentimes, in an attempt to find solutions, we find that the cost is more than the actual problem we're trying to solve. Save your time and energy for things that warrant your attention.

With parenthood comes a host of behaviors in need of addressing, but we must keep a perspective on the moments needing our full attention and authority.

This may require a bit of mindfulness on your part, but recall the question: How much does this *really* affect my life? How much does this *really* affect theirs? Pick your battles. Engaging with every minor annoyance will actually have an adverse effect on you. It won't feel empowering—you're often left worse for wear. Consider something as simple as road rage: do you really feel better after honking and swearing at someone that refused to use a blinker? It's unlikely.

Don't sweat the small stuff, keep small things small. Reducing the time and energy you spend on minor annoyances is an act of minimalism. Think of this practice as decluttering them off your radar. Only give air to things that are important to you, or those that will matter in the future.

 <u>**MINIMALIST MOM ACTION STEP:**</u> The next time you feel as though you may lose your temper with your child, take a step back. If the situation allows, step out of the room for a breather. Ask yourself, "Does this require a battle? Or can I let it slide?" Only you can define what is big or small in your life, but I'd be willing to guess there are specific behaviors that come to mind that aren't a big deal in the (parenting) long run.

**LET'S
SIMPLIFY:**
HOLIDAYS

HOLIDAY MINIMALISM

I don't know about you, but as any holiday approaches, the last thing I want to do is add extra stress to my plate.

As a mother, one of my deepest desires is for my children to look back upon their childhood with fond memories. I want them to one day reminisce on these holiday seasons and recreate the magic for their own families. But how much of the magic can be attributed to the "stuff" versus the experiences they enjoyed with family and friends? Here are a few reminders as you set up your holiday season:

1. **Keep expectations low**. Things aren't perfect. You can't predict everyone's actions or expectations. There are lots of people everywhere. Everyone wants to enjoy this time of year. Relieve the stress by recognizing that it's normal to feel overwhelmed during the holiday season. Simplify by choosing one thing you each want to do.

2. **Minimize your commitments**. A too-busy schedule causes stress. We underestimate how much we can pack into our schedules, especially as you add children to your family. You think you can get a lot done and then feel disappointed in yourself if you don't hit every item on the to-do list. Add time for more self-care and leisure. There are few things that bring me more joy than a snowy winter evening with a giant warm blanket, mug of something delicious, and a book (or re-run of *Downton Abbey*!).

3. Lastly (this isn't everywhere, but it is here in the Midwest), the weather is dark and cold. **Embrace it!** Look back to your childhood and ask yourself, in what ways did you most enjoy this weather? Create that experience with your children. Even if it's just thirty minutes. I know the stress of getting your children ready for the snow. It's almost as though you spend one hour getting ready for the snow, one hour in the snow, and one hour cleaning up. Your children will thank you, though.

TIPS FOR YOUR MINIMALIST THANKSGIVING

When it comes to Thanksgiving, what's the first thing that comes to mind? The scent of a twenty-pound turkey drifting through the halls, the sound of the hand mixer mashing potatoes, the clink of cheers being had round a table, the cheers of the crowd from the Macy's Day Parade? Thanksgiving is my all-time favorite holiday, so I don't want to skimp when it comes to celebrating. It'd be easy to go overboard, but simple is almost always better.

The preparation for Thanksgiving can entail countless hours of hard work and organizing. Here are four areas I'd suggest you focus on minimizing:

MENU

Most people can't get enough of traditional Thanksgiving Day foods. There are so many delicious recipes you could serve. My suggestion would be to simplify the menu by keeping it minimal (for example: turkey, yams and/or potatoes, a vegetable, gravy, rolls, stuffing, and dessert). Choose your favorite dishes and stick with those. Don't burden yourself with all the casseroles and pies you *could* be making. Cut down on the stress and keep the menu simple.

POTLUCK

Another way to simplify the evening would be to have each of your guests contribute a dish. Send a group text a couple of weeks before and have each guest "sign up" to bring something. Potlucks are typically a great way to simplify any gathering. Unless you love to cook, outsource!

Important note: Be sure to plan ahead. Don't wait until the day before to do your grocery shopping. It's likely that a majority of the items will be picked over and the stores packed. Be intentional with your time and planning. I'd also encourage you to rise a bit early on Thanksgiving to get the turkey in the oven, chop vegetables, and prep anything else you may need. Get yourself into the position where you can spend the majority of your holiday enjoying friends and family, not hunched over in the kitchen.

DÉCOR

Don't buy décor specifically for Thanksgiving, but generally for the harvest/autumnal season. This will allow you to keep your décor up for a longer period of time than just November. As for the actual decorations, I'd recommend bringing the outside in! Fall foliage lends itself to décor. Wood, leaves, pumpkins, gourds—these items can be found locally or at Trader Joe's for very affordable prices.

Another thing I love to do is have my children design the decorations. Have them pitch in to create placemats, name tags, and centerpieces. If you'd prefer to do it yourself, that's okay, too!

BLACK FRIDAY

Oh, Black Friday...I recall reading a quote from minimalist author Joshua Becker, "Only in America do we wait in line and trample each other for sale items one day after giving thanks for what we already have." How's that for irony?

In all seriousness, I understand that, for many, Black Friday is an enjoyable tradition to partake in. With that in mind, I say: change your tradition. Just kidding. But I would challenge you to rethink *how* you partake. My most radical suggestion would be to participate in a "buy nothing day" this year instead. Do you think you can do it? This is the ultimate minimalist approach created by individuals with a desire to protest consumerism.

For some, a "buy nothing day" may be considered blasphemous. That's totally okay. My suggestions for you, if you prefer to enjoy that day, would be:

1. **Shop online**. Why leave the comfort of your own home for a deal on that washing machine you need if you can get the same deal online?

2. **Head out around 8 a.m.** Crowds will sometimes die down before the later crowds come. A lot of shoppers have been out since 5–6 a.m., so you may be able to slip into a couple of stores without being bombarded by other shoppers.

3. This may be my most important tip: **take a friend or family member to keep you company in line**. Conversation with a friend plus getting a great deal equals multitasking at its finest.

I know that for many, Black Friday is a dear tradition. I understand that, but I'll also provide a reminder to *shop for what you need*. Remember: what is essential?

GRATITUDE

One of the most important tips I can give you is a reminder to remain grateful. Remember to focus on relational traditions, not materialism, and do so in a way that still keeps the holiday at the forefront. Practice thanksgiving for the many blessings you've been given throughout the year.

As you sit down to consume the meal, remember to go slow. Take your time. Sip your wine (or cider). Savor your food. Enjoy the time with one another as you share what you're most thankful for. How often are you around the table celebrating gratitude? It's perfectly fine to linger over this time with one another. It is your day off, after all. Treat it accordingly!

I can almost guarantee that if you have the resources to purchase this book, you have more resources than the majority of the world—give thanks!

A MINIMALIST CHRISTMAS

We are well into "that time of year" again. You know the one. Toward the end of August, we walk into stores only to be hit with hints of the holidays to come. One week it's a witch's hat and floating ghost, the next it's a Christmas tree and moving reindeer. Marketers are pushier than ever during this time. It isn't enough to buy twinkle lights for your house; now you *must* buy ones that flash various colors, and a blow-up Santa for your lawn. We're being bombarded with advertisements (and let's be honest, our children's irrational input). It's hard to be decisive and intentional when it comes to holiday decorating. In this section, my hope is to help you simplify and remove some of the guesswork when adding that touch of holiday cheer to your space.

Before you walk down the path of overwhelm at the beginning of October, remember control what you *can*. If the idea of a minimalist holiday season is new to you, begin to implement new traditions and expectations for the entire family. Don't overwhelm yourself—you don't have to make "all the changes" this year. Small changes will be felt, too. On the bright side, if you've already begun to minimize and remove clutter from your home, you'll have the space (and time) to add new things.

There's nothing worse than adding more clutter to an already cluttered home.

GIFT-GIVING

> Ask yourself these questions: Who's in charge of the Christmas list? Are the decisions being made between you and your spouse/partner, or does one of you take charge? What will feel too excessive? What fits with your goals for the future?

I've mentally wrestled with the best way to approach gift-giving, but when I consider what to gift, I come back to these options: something to wear, something to read, something you want, and something you need. Have you ever heard of this? In my family we call it the "four gift rule." I'd actually heard of it prior to beginning the *Minimalist Moms Podcast* and thought it was a great way to reduce the number of toys we'd have each holiday. Growing up, I never lacked presents on holidays (that's putting it lightly). I'm so grateful to have been loved—even nowadays, still loved—in that way. However, in an effort to save money and focus on traditions, my husband and I decided on the "four gift rule." One of the gifts may be a "big-ticket" item, or maybe they all are, but that's the fun of it! You can adapt and shift as your children grow. It's great because you know what to expect as you craft your list and what to be on the lookout for when you shop, so it doesn't take nearly as long to get everything done.

I mentioned at the beginning that gifting is something I've wrestled with. I won't lie to you and say it always feels easy. Looking back on photos of our most recent Christmas and seeing my five-year old daughter looking at her four gifts, I began to second guess myself. We'd celebrated with my husband's family on Christmas Eve and she had already received a great deal of gifts hours before, so I was worried that mine didn't stand out. I wondered if I could've wrapped them better. Were they "exciting" enough?

Do you hear how unhealthy this inner dialogue is? I felt guilty about the amount of Christmas presents I'd given my child.

Talk about a "first world problem." I'm not mentioning this to minimize these emotions if you have them; only to emphasize that I was projecting my programmed mind (even still) of "not enough." Reader, she had enough. She *has* enough. Christmas is a wonderful time to show our love through gift-giving, but it's not the *only* reason we celebrate. Our children receive gifts all year long. Birthdays, celebrations, little gifts here and there—there are plenty of opportunities for our children to be showered with gifts.

We need to kick this mindset out, focus on long-term goals, and create a game plan. Write out every person you need to buy for and the maximum amount you are able to spend. I suggest not planning alone if you have a significant other. Your partner may love to shop and find deals, or you can divide tasks based on preferences. For my husband and I, planning ahead is huge for our overall annual budgeting. You may have a system (or need to create a system) that incorporates the holiday season.

In the early years of our marriage, my husband and I bought one of my most favorite gifts. We chose not to buy individual gifts and instead purchased a weekend getaway in a cabin for his side of the family. Every couple we invited—I believe there were eight couples including ourselves—provided a meal throughout the weekend. This made the holiday much less expensive overall and provided an experience that was well worth the cost. We chose to do this because I found that the hardest thing about buying for older people is that they may have everything they "need." I don't want to exchange money to just exchange money. If you're all on board (or if the majority of your extended family is), save your energy and enjoy spending time together celebrating this glorious time of year.

Remember that *you* still control what you give to your kids. You may not be able to fully control what others gift your family, but if you want to pare down, no one is stopping you! We never want to take away the opportunity of expressing love through gifts. Joshua Becker suggests steering others into what you'd like to receive by "[prioritizing] quality over quantity, needs over wants, consumables over clutter, gift lists, and experiences [you'd like your children to have]." Grandparents usually don't heed to your requests the first time, but after a while, they'll catch on.

How Do I Handle Gifts I Didn't Ask For?

People are excited to show their love by giving-gifts, especially during the holiday season. But what happens when you receive something that you didn't ask for or want? Knowing how to accept graciously is a skill we all should hone. It should be your goal to respond in such a way that the gift-giver knows you genuinely appreciate the gesture (even if the sweater is itchy or the perfume isn't your signature scent).

I'll preface this section by stating that it's never my intention to discredit the generosity of a well-intended family member. However, it's important to stick to your perspective when it comes to the toy/gift inventory associated with outside gifting.

A quick fact for you: according to research in *Life at Home in the Twenty-First Century*, "other relatives contribute to children's material assemblages, including about $500 spent by grandparents each year on toys, clothes, books, and other gifts." Even if you're intentional about setting boundaries and providing wish lists, we all have a relative (or two) that desires to buy off the list. Know that you're not alone in navigating this tricky situation—I've found this to be a struggle in my own life. As for how to handle it, I have a couple of ideas.

First and foremost: as a recipient, no matter how ridiculous the gift may be, it's your job to accept it graciously. Remember that the gift-giver never has negative intent. Don't assume that they're trying to go against your wishes, they may just express love differently than you.

I believe it's completely fine to accept the gift graciously but ask for a receipt to return certain items. For example, for Christmas one year, my son received a basketball hoop that we already owned. Therefore, I didn't feel guilty when mentioning that fact to the gift-giver. I kindly thanked them for the item and then stated why I wouldn't need to keep it.

Another example from that same year was when my daughter received a red sweater dress similar to one she already owned. I mentioned this to the giver and they happily offered to return it and purchase something different.

This can get tricky, though, when you receive an item you simply don't want or need. Most givers include a gift receipt to avoid awkward "This doesn't fit," "It's not my color," or "I don't like this" situations. If the receipt isn't included, how you move forward will depend on the relationship you have with the giver. If you're close with one another, they'll likely understand; if you're not as close, it may be best to say "thank you" and think about what to do the following day. If there's a real chance that the giver may be personally offended, I'd suggest returning the gift on your own (if you can) and keeping the information to yourself.

If you're unable to find/obtain the receipt, I'd do one of two things:

1. If you're aware of where the giver purchased the item, call the store and speak with the manager to see if store credit is something you're able to exchange for the item. You most likely won't receive cash back, but you may be able to gain credit toward something you'd prefer. Be sure not to wait too long after the gift was given, as

seasons change quickly in stores. You want to ensure the likelihood that your item will be taken back.

2. If this path doesn't work, then I suggest selling, donating, or re-gifting the item on your own terms. These option are resourceful, sustainable, and leave the giver unoffended.

A Note on Travel Gift-Gifting

I'm regularly asked what type of gift (if any) parents should bring to their children when coming home from a getaway trip. I think it's a really great question and figured a lot of people may be wondering how to minimize this area of unnecessary gift-giving. My advice: skip the gift. Instead, make your return home genuine and intentional. Give your child a really big hug and express to them how much they were missed. Tell them you'd love to spend some quality time together to catch up. Even if you have an older teen, you could go grab a coffee from the drive-through together. Don't feel guilty for the lack of a gift. The time away was about you (or you and your significant other). A gift is a symbol that represents the fact that you thought about/were missing someone during your time away. Instead, speak these things directly to them. If you are someone who truly does love to give a gift, I suggest consumables over clutter.

QUICK TIPS FOR A SMOOTHER HOLIDAY SEASON

- Plan ahead!

- Organize a Secret Santa for extended family members/coworkers (buy only one gift).

- Practice the "rule of four," addressing Wear/Read/ Want/Need vs. overabundance from Santa.

- Give gifts that focus on an experience or hobby (e.g., shoes or a leotard for a ballet dancer, a bathing suit or goggles for a swimmer).

- Give homemade gifts to teachers, friends, and coworkers.

- Think: what do "grownups" want? Time/experiences/ fancy food/charity donations/nothing.

WHEN OTHERS WANT TO BUY FOR YOU...

- Have a list ready.

- Have your discussion ready. No matter how much you try to say "no," certain individuals will still want to buy you gifts. I find it easier when I have a discussion ready for these moments. Try telling them, "I've been thinking a lot the past few months about how stressful the holidays are now compared to when we were kids. This year I'm going to try to shift my focus to family, good food, and fun, rather than physical gifts, so there's no need to buy me anything this year."

HOLIDAY DECORATION & PREPARATION

Before you begin the holiday decoration process, take stock of what you own—the old and the new. As always, use intentionality when making decisions. I highly encourage you to make a list of what you have versus what you need to buy.

Ideas for Decorating the Inside of Your Home

1. **Previous holiday artwork:** Do you have artwork from when your little one was in preschool? It may be fun to pull some out and place it on display.

2. **DIY crafts:** Time to tap into your crafty side. Try creating a DIY Advent tray, banner, or cardboard cutouts of a Christmas tree, or other appropriate symbol. This is a great way to get in the holiday spirit while saving money on something you can make yourself.

3. **Candles:** A lovely, *hygge*-inspired way to decorate your space. Who doesn't love to smell cinnamon, balsam, or cedar when they step foot into a home?

4. **Wrap frames in paper:** Another idea for decorating on a dime you may have seen before.

5. **Wall tree:** This might be a reach, but if you really want to simplify this year, try a wall tree. Line up branches or lights on your wall and create this minimalist décor.

6. **Decorate with festive books.**

7. **Bring the outdoors inside:** Decorate with pine, branches, pinecones from parks, or seek out ideas on Pinterest/the internet.

8. **Wrap gifts in brown paper "tied up with string" or fabric:** This looks lovely underneath the tree.

Ideas for Decorating the Outside of Your Home

1. **Wreath(s):** Adding this touch of flair to the outside of your home is an inexpensive way to decorate. Creating your own from compostable materials is a resourceful way to use what you have, but investing in a nice wreath

you can use year after year embraces the idea of quality discussed earlier in the book. I've also seen homemade "half" wreaths, a unique spin on this traditional decoration. (If you've never heard of this, a quick Google search will show you how to create one of your own!)

2. **Candles in windows:** There's something so magical about candles in the window. I wouldn't suggest an open flame, but you can set a timer to turn electric candles on at sundown. It makes a huge difference in your home's appearance.
3. **Garland on the porch.**
4. **Fairy lights.**

ENJOYING THE SEASON

You don't have to spend a fortune to enjoy the magic of this season. Here are some of my favorite, inexpensive ways to celebrate:

- Bake homemade cookies with children or friends.
- Cookie exchange: Take cookie baking a step further by hosting or scheduling a cookie exchange, where each guest brings a different platter of cookies to share with one another's families.
- Grab a cup of hot chocolate from a local cafe and drive around town to look at the lights. Christmas tunes are a

must. We love to seek out surrounding neighborhoods that have large displays.

- Hike in the woods on a snowy morning. Bring a thermos of soup to share!

- Ask around about/seek out free events happening in your city. We have an amazing Christmas train display at the main library in town. My children love to see this year after year.

- Host (or organize) a holiday-themed movie night. Potluck style is always the way to go—unless hosting is your thing, then go for that! *It's a Wonderful Life*, *White Christmas*, *A Christmas Story*, *Home Alone*, *The Family Stone* (is this really a Christmas movie?)—I like to choose one most of us have already seen so we can catch up a bit while we watch. Enjoy with snacks, spiced cider, or wine.

- Host (or organize) for your children and their friends. We like to stay in our jammies for this party each year.

- Decorate gingerbread houses with your children. If the kits are too pricey, graham crackers and homemade icing work well, too!

I'd love to see how you've chosen to celebrate the holidays in a minimalist way this year! Use the hashtag #minimalistmoms on Instagram to share your celebrations with our community.

LET'S SIMPLIFY:
POST-HOLIDAY
DECLUTTERING

The day after Christmas haze. You know it. Wrapping paper scattered here and there. A half-eaten Christmas pie still on the dining room table (breakfast, anyone?). You only have a handful of days left in the year, so let's use this section to gain some encouragement for post-holiday decluttering. Take advantage of this special time of year—a lot of people may not have work, or may be able to utilize help from children who are home on holiday break. Whatever the case may be, I'm here to assist you with a few tips as you calm the chaos of the holidays!

I wouldn't say there is any particular order to addressing these post-holiday decluttering tips, so feel free to dive in wherever seems best.

- **Declutter the kitchen!** Open up the fridge: do you have leftovers from Christmas? It's time to toss anything that isn't going to be eaten or has passed its consumption date. Think about the wine. Do you have any left over? Most wine will only keep for about five to seven days once opened, as it begins to oxidize. So pour that down the drain if it's past its prime—it's only taking up precious space in your fridge.

- **Organize the pantry.** Figure out what has expired, and if there's food in there you don't intend on eating, go ahead and donate or toss it. This is a good time to clear out and get ready for any health and fitness goals you may have for the upcoming year.

- **Clean up the extra boxes lying around.** Do you have Christmas packages lingering under the tree that need to be picked up? What about empty Amazon boxes in the basement? Do a walk-through and recycle/ toss anything that needs to leave the space. Our recycling bin is completely filled to the brim in the days after Christmas.

- Along the same lines as Christmas boxes, **what about Christmas catalogs?** Pop those in the recycling bin. You don't want those hanging around, as they may only encourage attitudes of ungratefulness. Your kids (and maybe you) may see something they didn't receive and end up whining about it. Best to just toss!

- My next tip would be, as you clean up holiday décor, immediately **get rid of anything that has seen better**

Let's Simplify: Post-Holiday Decluttering

days. For us, we had a couple of ornaments that were worse for the wear. These probably couldn't be fixed with even the strongest of glue, so we just had to say goodbye to them and put the others back in the bin. There's no point in storing these items for another eleven months, only to pull them out next year and toss them then. I'd also encourage you to look through your holiday boxes to see what you can part with. What didn't you pull out this year? Why? Has your style changed? If you are only keeping the item for sentimental reasons, remind yourself of these points: Sentimentality is as emotion. The pull is so strong, but many times it's not rational or even helpful. Pause to consider what emotion is tugging on you. Is it positive or negative? Is it a weight or is it uplifting? Make sure the memories attached are good ones. Don't hold on to stuff out of obligation or guilt.

- **Christmas cards**. I know they often carry a lot of sentimental value for people. If this describes you, I would say hole punch each card and store them on a ring so you can flip through them year after year and see how people have grown. You could also take a picture of the wall/space where you store them and keep that photo in your yearly scrapbook. Just remember, if you choose to keep Christmas cards, ask yourself if you really plan on going back and looking through them. Have you done that already?

- My last tip: **focus on old toys**. This is an area where you can involve the kids. What toys do you have that are broken or have missing pieces? There's no sense in keeping these ones if they're only taking up room in the toy box or on the shelf. Next, ask your kids what they play with. You could actually use this as an experiment—I did myself! On Christmas Eve, I gave Charlotte a cardboard box and told her to remove anything from her room she didn't want to play with anymore. Twenty minutes later, she pushed a full box out into the living room. I couldn't believe it. I don't think this would necessarily work with every child, but I explained to her that she would be getting new presents that night and that it'd be great if she could donate some of her toys to children that didn't have any (or that were looking for something she may have but doesn't want anymore).

If your child is struggling with this or isn't old enough to help quite yet, go through and be really honest about what they do and don't play with anymore. If it's something a future child would play with, then I'd say to hold off on purging. However, if you don't plan on having any more children, as Marie Kondo would say, thank the item for its service and get rid of it!

DECLUTTERING YOUR CLOSET

Can I make a suggestion? Hold off on decluttering your closet until February. Maybe it's just me, but I tend to come out of the holiday season slightly more bloated than normal. If I were to begin the decluttering process on my wardrobe, I may rid my closet of items that will fit better a few months post-holiday season. Save the wardrobe pare down for spring cleaning.

You may be surprised, but I like to keep our Christmas tree up through the majority of January. I strip it of its ornaments and leave the twinkle lights on to sparkle through that first long, dark month of winter. I know a lot of you prefer to completely clean up your space after the holiday season, but keeping the tree around slightly longer makes me happy.

SIMPLIFYING THE HOLIDAY SEASON: WHAT EVERYDAY MINIMALIST MOMS ARE SAYING

Jacq: We choose experiences (especially trips) over presents!

Elizabeth: Choose four gifts total: something you wear, read, want, and need. Sometimes, I'll allow the "want" to be a big-ticket item!

Tesha: Give a list to family members with exactly what you would like. I keep a running list throughout the year of things I would like, but don't necessarily need. This way, I'm prepared when the holidays arrive.

Emily: My best advice for the holidays is to set expectations about gifts early. I typically send a list to our family in September.

Corenia: On the day of celebration, note what resonates with you and where you feel off/frustrated/ tired. Then, make a physical note on a post-it and place it in your planner for next year (around November 1st.) I do this and it reminds me to only give energy to the things we love as a family. Since starting this tradition, we reflect on our highlights together. It makes celebrations more of an "us" experience.

Candi: It's good to attempt minimalist gifting ideas (like zoo memberships, fewer toys, etc.), but don't guilt yourself when your child is still given too much from others (i.e., family). Move forward with confidence knowing that you will work through previous toys along with what is given.

Ali: During the holiday season, I keep these things in mind like a mantra: "This year, I'm going to decline participating in holiday traditions that leave me feeling exhausted, empty, and overwhelmed. This year, I'm going to stop living outdated expectations of the holidays. This year, I'm going to support a simple, mindful, meaningful holiday where we focus on both connecting with loved ones and connecting with the spirit of Christmas."

Each year, I vow more and more strongly to break away from the cycle of giving, for its effects are short-lived. We should be giving each other long-lasting love, time, and experiences, rather than objects that are only momentarily important. However, when it comes to grandparents giving my son, my husband, and me gifts, I can only remind them once that we'd rather have experiences or donations to college funds. They never remember, and we have to consider how their version of gift-giving is different. They really feel like they are "giving love" with each gift. We thank them and then find a way to regift or sell the items.

Elissa: I'm trying something new this year: a Christmas greeting video, carol sing-along style. Time capsule moment and zero paper and postage.

Nicole: On Thanksgiving, we always serve dinner potluck style. This keeps me from standing over the stove all day and enables me to interact with guests, which is really my favorite part of the day!

Ashlee: Remember: You don't have to go. If you go, you don't have to pass your baby around. If you pass the baby around, you can take them back at any time. And you don't have to stay late.

BECOMING A MINIMALIST MOM: HAVE YOURSELF A MINIMALIST HOLIDAY SEASON

What is one initial step you can implement to slow down your holiday season?

_____

_____

_____

_____

_____

_____

_____

Brainstorm experiential gifts you could give instead of possessions.

_____

_____

_____

_____

_____

_____

_____

Let's Simplify: Post-Holiday Decluttering

How will you simplify your decorations?

_____

_____

_____

_____

_____

_____

_____

_____

What outing/activity will you prioritize over others?
(Remember to cut down on what you "should" do and
prioritize what you and your family "desire" to do!)

_____

_____

_____

_____

_____

_____

_____

_____

Brainstorm: How could you preserve the memory of an item while still letting it go?

_____

_____

_____

_____

_____

_____

_____

_____

LET'S
SIMPLIFY:
WASTE

ECO-MINIMALISM

What first comes to mind when you think of sustainability? I used to imagine one of two images:

1. Large recycling bins you'd load up throughout the week and set at the curb on Monday morning.
2. A burlap-wearing, stainless-steel-water-bottle-toting individual I might see in Whole Foods.

I'm sure many who are new to this concept will think the same. Sustainability and minimalism, however, are areas that go hand in hand. When you choose minimalism, you are also choosing a more sustainable way of life as well. Consumerism is the biggest cause of harm to our planet. It depletes resources and encourages the toxic cycle of buying and eventually dumping no-longer-wanted items in landfills. If you buy less, and use only what you need, you will be doing the planet a huge favor (and your wallet, too).

Merriam-Webster defines sustainable as, "of, relating to, or being a method of harvesting or using a resource so that the resource is not depleted or permanently damaged."

I'm not sure about you, but when I first began investigating what it'd be like to live a sustainable lifestyle, I was completely overwhelmed. I knew I wanted to create a more eco-friendly home for my family, but wasn't exactly sure where to start. I remember initially doing a Google search and stumbling upon a woman who literally kept all of her trash *for a year* in one small glass jar. No joke. One small glass jar (her name is Lauren Singer and I find that quite amazing, by the way). All that to say, while her accomplishment is amazing, the probability of implementing those changes in a family home seemed unlikely for the everyday person.

But living a sustainable lifestyle isn't impossible. We can absolutely make small changes and start living with consideration of our current resources and a future-oriented mindset.

At the time I began seeking out more information on sustainability, my podcast co-host and I decided to find someone to interview on the topic. We wanted a mother who could make sustainability and zero-waste living seem within reach. A local mother who led a community zero-waste movement joined us on the podcast and discussed all of the ways she was living out the lifestyle. She discussed the importance of buying in bulk, carrying reusable bags, bicycling, and using handkerchiefs, reusable razors, and menstrual cups. These were things I could implement in my life. (I apologize to Lauren Singer, but I'm just not sure one jar of trash per year is in the cards for my household.)

But the question on my mind still needed to be answered…how do I do this with children?

In April of 2019, I had the amazing opportunity to interview mother and zero-waste leader Bea Johnson on the *Minimalist Moms Podcast*. It was an educational moment, but after our conversation, I was still left feeling overwhelmed. It seemed like living sustainably and producing zero waste would encompass an entire lifestyle change. I felt like the changes I'd already implemented to this point were helpful, but I still felt as though there was *so* much more I could be doing.

As I've had more of a chance to continue pursuing this lifestyle shift, I've seen that there are things that have come easier than expected, while other compromises I'm just not quite willing to make. I tend to be black and white in my thinking—it's usually all or nothing for me. But acknowledging the gray in this area could make a significant impact.

I knew that I wanted to include a section on sustainability in this book because of its importance to our environment, but I also wanted to include it because of the potential effect mothers can have when teaching future generations. As with minimalism, everyone's approach to zero-waste is going to look different. I wanted to encourage that taking small steps is still better than nothing. Zero-waste chef Anne-Marie Bonneau said it best:

"We don't need a handful of people doing zero waste perfectly. We need millions of people doing it imperfectly."

Here are some ways I've begun to incorporate more sustainable, zero-waste methods into my home:

- **Reusable water bottles**: You guys, this is such an easy switch (and honestly, I prefer using these to tote water than rickety, cheap, plastic bottles). I purchased two bottles at Costco for around ten dollars and ended up going back for two more, so each member of my family could have their own. We use them all day, every day. Not only are disposable water bottles not great for the environment, but the cost adds up over time—even if it seems like only a couple hundred dollars a year, think of what else you could do with that money. I love that I can refill my water bottle when I'm at the zoo and save five dollars on overpriced bottled water. If you can't be

convinced of the environmental factor, the financial savings alone are worthwhile.

- **Reusable grocery bags**: Super inexpensive to purchase and so much sturdier than plastic or paper bags. I also love that a lot of grocery stores take a small percentage off your grocery bill for using these. Trader Joe's even has a weekly giveaway for anyone using reusable bags! I store mine in the side panel of my door so I remember to grab them as I exit my vehicle.

- **To-go/reusable coffee mugs**: As with the water bottles, you can carry a transportable coffee mug. People have been doing this for years (probably without realizing how beneficial it is for the environment). If you're not making coffee at home, most coffee shops will fill your cup, no questions asked. Just be sure to mention it as you're placing your order. Another bonus is that with a portable coffee mug, you don't have to worry about straws or plastic lids (which always seem to fall off anyway). Win-win.

- **Paperless bills/receipts/magazines**: This is an easy shift that takes little time on your part.

- **Reusable straws**: It may take some time to remember to bring your straw with you, but I just throw mine in my purse and use it as needed.

- **Glass food storage containers**: I love the versatility of glass containers (as opposed to disposable, plastic Tupperware). You can freeze them, microwave them, and use them to store leftovers. I also send them to school with my children—they just have to remember to bring them back! Ugh!

- **Using a handkerchief instead of Kleenex**: This may not be for everyone, but I'm all about bringing back the handkerchief.
- **Recycling**: Be sure to check what your city will accept—sometimes throwing your plastic bags in there actually causes more damage than good. Take plastic bags to grocery store recycling bins, as they can clog up your local recycling system conveyor belts.
- **Menstrual cup**: Okay, so I haven't used one of these yet, but I have friends that swear by them. Once I'm out of the season of pregnancy and nursing, I plan to check it out for myself.

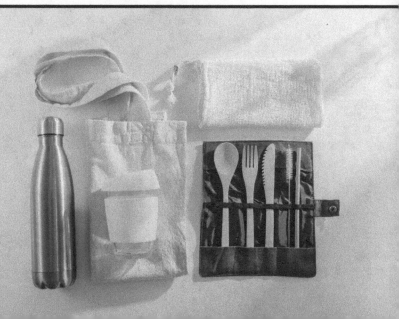

- **Opt for the cone** instead of a cup at the ice cream shop (ha—had to include this one for all of my sweet tooth buddies!). You could also take a mason jar or another type of glass container instead.

This list is small and there are more ways I could be contributing to the environment, but I wanted you to have an honest view of the things I'm able to manage as a mother of three.

What sustainable changes have you made to your household? Use the hashtag #minimalistmoms on Instagram to share with our community.

BUT WHAT DOES SUSTAINABILITY LOOK LIKE IN MY CHILDREN'S LIVES?

It's tough. I'm not going to act as though this area is always smooth sailing, or that we don't still contribute waste. I will say that I have made considerable strides in this area and my children are starting to catch on (at least my oldest is).

IDEAS FOR SUSTAINABLE MINIMALISM WITH KIDS

- **Toys from the dentist/doctor's office:** This is tricky to avoid, but I typically try to bring a snack of our own to entice my children at the end of the visit. I don't mind if they take a sucker or piece of candy, but I try to avoid the little plastic toys as much as possible.

- **Build a package-free pantry:** Even before I started making more environmentally conscious choices, I was on board with buying products that contained as little waste as possible. I prefer to create my own granola bars. I serve bulk seeds, nuts, and dried fruit as snacks. Try purchasing a large chunk of cheese instead of cheese sticks. Refrain from serving applesauce pouches when you can make your own from scratch (or purchase a jar instead, which is also more cost efficient!).

- **Birthday parties:**
  - I don't want to come off as a Scrooge, but is there really a parent who *loves* the goodie bags associated with birthday parties? They are a pain to put together, and really just seem like a waste of money that could've been spent elsewhere.
  - I appreciate this quote from zero-waste devotee Bea Johnson: "I'm not suggesting that your kids refuse them all, doing so would require superpowers. But I am hopeful that they will consider the disposal and impact of taking these objects. You will be amazed at how much clutter they will keep from coming in ..." As with everything, talk to your kids about this! You'll be surprised at their can-do attitudes when it comes to keeping clutter at bay.
  - While you may not be able to control the goodie bag your child brings home, you certainly can take charge in your own home. My first suggestion is to send guests home with a perishable item instead of a bag full of plastic knickknacks. My cousin once sent jars of jam home with each guest for her son's birthday party. You could also send home succulents, flowers, seeds to plant, small bags of coffee, something locally made—really anything that isn't going to immediately end up lost in your car or go straight to the landfill.
  - Consider the birthday theme. What could you send that aligns with your theme? I once attended a

lumberjack themed birthday and all of the guests
went home with a small jar of local honey.

- Send home an extra cupcake for later and skip the
  toys if you can.
- Choose paper bags over plastic for transport.

- **More digital work and less paperwork:** Ask your child's
  teacher to make this switch. It may not be possible,
  but it also doesn't hurt to ask. I told my daughter's
  preschool teacher to never include a monthly schedule
  in her mailbox. I simply took a picture of the main copy
  at the classroom door each month! I plugged in the
  essential dates and deleted the photo when it was no
  longer needed.

- **Water bottles at sporting events:** Again, just have your
  child take their own water bottle and encourage the
  coach to have others do the same.

For further information on sustainability, check out the
following resources (preferably from a library or sec-
ondhand book shop): *The Sustainable(ish) Living Guide:
Everything You Need to Know to Make Small Changes that
Make a Big Difference* by Jen Gale, *Attainable Sustainable:
The Lost Art of Self-Reliant Living* by Kris Bordessa, and
*Zero Waste Home: The Ultimate Guide to Simplifying Your
Life by Reducing Your Waste* by Bea Johnson (this one is
a *daunting*, but fascinating read).

Please hear me when I say: I do not do any of this 100 percent of the time. My intentionality wanes in more stressful seasons, but my goal is to do *something*. I try to do the best I can with the mental and physical resources I have. Don't forget Anne-Marie Bonneau's words, **"We don't need a handful of people doing zero waste perfectly. We need millions of people doing it imperfectly."** You can do this!

SUSTAINABLE LIVING: WHAT EVERYDAY MINIMALIST MOMS ARE SAYING

Brittany: Don't go out and buy "sustainable" products. You're giving in to a market that doesn't always have sustainability in mind. The most sustainable and minimal thing you can do is use what you have first. Give your butter container a rinse and pack lunch in it the next day!

Candi: The most helpful "mantra" for our family that I've heard and deeply believe is that our world doesn't need families striving for perfection with sustainability, but more families striving imperfectly towards small and attainable goals for sustainability.

Emily: Seek to understand the hands and hearts behind what you buy. Many companies state their sustainability practices and other important practices (labor, charitable giving, etc.) on their websites. Seek out companies that are good to the people who work for them, are good to the earth, and good to others in the community. Resources like The Good Trade are helpful to find these kinds of companies.

Sara: There have been numerous things that have aided my sustainability practice:

- Take a to-go kit with you when you're out and about. Tiffin, jar, utensils, napkin, canvas bag. Have one set per person in your family.

- If you're driving somewhere with your kids, pack a growler with ice water to refill their reusable cups.

- Pack food and your to-go kit when you take road trips. You can eat at rest stops, your kids can run around, and you can make more sustainable food choices then fast food.

- Purchase in bulk and when you're at the grocery store and refill your own containers.

- Meal plan and then go to the farmers market to get ingredients. Be flexible. You can make a lot less waste and support local business.

- Thrift, swap, or borrow clothes for your kids when they are young. When they get older and want to choose their clothes, take them thrifting or set up a swap with their friends. Make it a party.

- Don't go overboard for parties. Use real plates, cups, and silverware.

- It's mostly about thinking ahead. Choosing to refuse, reduce, and reuse!

Let's Simplify: Waste

BECOMING A MINIMALIST MOM: SUSTAINABLE PRACTICES FOR THE WHOLE FAMILY

Brainstorm: In what ways could you make your home more sustainable?

_____

_____

_____

_____

_____

_____

_____

_____

_____

_____

_____

_____

_____

_____

_____

_____

Brainstorm: What changes could you make to
consume more consciously/sustainably?

_____

_____

_____

_____

_____

_____

_____

Baby steps: What is the first way you plan to
implement more sustainable living for your family?

_____

_____

_____

_____

_____

_____

_____

Who do you know that is one step ahead of you on
this journey? How could you reach out to them to
assist you as you continue to make changes?

_____

_____

_____

_____

_____

_____

_____

_____

How can you apply a more sustainable mindset
specifically when it comes to your children? Parties?
Sports? School environment?

_____

_____

_____

_____

_____

_____

_____

_____

YOU'RE BECOMING A MINIMALIST

FINAL WORDS OF ENCOURAGEMENT

Alright, you've made it through the book. How are you feeling? Are you better prepared to start tackling areas of your life that need some simplifying? It is my hope that you're able to take some of these tips that have worked in my life and implement them in your own, even if our journeys look a little different. As I said when we began our time together, minimalism isn't a place you "arrive" at, but a journey through your life. Throughout the various ages of your children, and then the inevitable empty nester state, I'm sure that minimalism will look different. The days of toy clutter will shift into structure throughout your home.

It is also my hope that the areas of focus have encouraged you on your minimalist journey. Not one person reading this book will be at the same stage of this journey. These areas are intended to meet you in whatever season you find yourself— some may even seem contradictory to one another depending on what you're most needing in life.

As you begin (or continue to pursue) your journey of minimalist living, try not to compare yourself to others. Just because that influencer on Instagram has pristine white walls, thirty items in their capsule wardrobe, and labels on every individual pantry item doesn't mean that will work in your life. Minimalism is a tool. Use it to get rid of items that you deem unnecessary and continue to question what is essential throughout your lifetime.

SUGGESTED RESOURCES

HELPFUL TOOLS I'VE FOUND THROUGHOUT MY MINIMALIST JOURNEY

These resources have had a profound influence in my minimalist pursuits. If you'd like more wisdom as you continue to pursue minimalism, you might enjoy these books.

BOOKS

- ***Simplicity Parenting: Using the Extraordinary Power of Less to Raise Calmer, Happier, and More Secure Kids*, by Kim John Payne, with Lisa M. Ross**. This is one of the first books I always recommend to individuals that desire to implement a more minimalist, intentional approach to parenting. Payne's philosophy is to slow down and give your child the space to be themselves. Stop crowding their space with "stuff" and "noise" (literally, too much noise throughout the day is proven to have negative effects on our minds). This is an informative, quick read that will transform the way you parent.

- ***Soulful Simplicity: How Living with Less Can Lead to So Much More*, by Courtney Carver**. Another OG in the minimalist community. *Soulful Simplicity* is an absolute game changer. There are many books on the market that discuss decluttering and minimalism, but this reads as more of a guide to simplifying your soul. It's deep, but accessible.

- ***Chasing Slow: Courage to Journey Off the Beaten Path*, by Erin Loechner**. As a woman in pursuit of minimalism and slow living, I was convinced by Loechner's statement: "I do not yet realize that, without grace, pursuing the slow life is just as exhausting as pursuing the fast one. Without grace, minimalism is another metric for perfection. Chasing slow is still a chase." Chasing slow is still a chase. But how do we stop? This is one of those books you'll return to throughout your life due to the sheer beauty of the writing and the spot-on perception of our fast-paced culture. Loechner is also the founder of Other Goose, the homeschooling strategy that is all-inclusive and "values play, freedom and structure." This venture is yet another creation of her "slow down" mentality.

- ***Digital Minimalism: Choosing a Focused Life in a Noisy World*, by Cal Newport**. This book doesn't just touch on the "how" or "what" to digitally eliminate, it provides practical suggestions for creating space for in your life for what you really want. The topic can feel overwhelming, but Newport provides strong evidence on why we feel so addicted to technology (specifically, social media) and why it's in our best interest to make an effort to break these habits.

- ***How to Break Up with Your Phone: The 30-Day Plan to Take Back Your Life*, by Catherine Price**. In this day and age, it's difficult *not* to feel attached to your phone. As mothers, we have to remember that our children are watching and repeating our behaviors. This book encouraged me to set boundaries around my phone— when to use it and where to store it. This is a quick read that could be life-changing for many. I've tried "fasting" from my phone (twenty-four hours, once a week) and felt great freedom from the separation. Our phones are designed to be addictive, and the time we spend on them affects our ability to focus and connect with those around us. It's curious how we can have access to so many individuals, yet a great deal of our society remarks that they've never been more lonely. Price gives detailed, approachable tips to "break up" with our phones for good.

- ***Rhythms of Renewal: Trading Stress and Anxiety for a Life of Peace and Purpose*, by Rebekah Lyons**. Lyons probably wouldn't define herself as a minimalist, but so much of this book is about slow, intentional living. She discusses four "rhythms": rest, restore, connect, and create. This would be a great place to start for individuals looking to implement routines and rhythms in their lives.

- ***The Minimalist Home: A Room-by-Room Guide to a Decluttered, Refocused Life*, by Joshua Becker**. A practical, step-by-step guide to decluttering your home.

- ***Better Than Before*, by Gretchen Rubin**. There is no one-size-fits-all when it comes to adopting new habits, as we all have different personal tendencies. After reading this, I felt motivated to tackle some areas of my life that needed to get back on track. This is one of those books that I regularly re-read. I checked it out from the library, but plan to buy a copy for my personal bookshelf.

- ***Have Yourself a Minimalist Christmas: Slow Down, Save Money & Enjoy a More Intentional Holiday*, by Meg Nordmann**. There is no other book like this on the market! This is a must-read, not only for minimalists, but for anyone looking to slow down and simplify their holiday season.

- ***Sabbath: Finding Rest, Renewal, and Delight in Our Busy Lives*, by Wayne Muller**. A much broader approach to the idea of Sabbath. As opposed to limiting it to one specific day, Muller provides a convincing spiritual argument for taking a regular Sabbath. (I use the word "spiritual" as I wouldn't say it's overly Christian. He incorporates Buddhist philosophies, as well.)

- ***Life at Home in the Twenty-First Century: 32 Families Open Their Doors*, by Jeanne E. Arnold, Anthony P. Graesch, Enzo Ragazzini, and Elinor Ochs**. This is a fascinating photographic exploration of what thirty-two typical, American middle-class family homes look like, and what the images say about contemporary life. This book sets the groundwork for minimalist habits that we have covered.

- **There's No Such Thing as Bad Weather: A Scandinavian Mom's Secrets for Raising Healthy, Resilient, and Confident Kids (from Friluftsliv to Hygge), by Linda Åkeson McGurk**. This book was a pivotal read for me in simplifying my parenting. I've always loved being in nature, but struggled to push my family outside during weather "extremes." McGurk presents the Scandinavian philosophy that there really is "no such thing as bad weather," rather, you're just unprepared for the circumstances. This is a beautiful blend of memoir and research that has inspired me to change my attitude regarding nature and dirt. While I was already a firm believer in getting children outside, I was hesitant to get them too dirty and placed boundaries on their exploration. This book has reassured me that they will be just fine (and will even benefit) from less restraint on my part. My unnatural efforts to keep them "clean" and under control only undermine their ability to learn and understand the world.

WEBSITES

- Becoming Minimalist, by Joshua Becker
- Be More with Less, by Courtney Carver
- Gretchen Rubin's self-titled website
- The Good Trade, a sustainable resource

PODCASTS

- *Minimalist Moms Podcast*, hosted by Diane Boden
- *With Intention* (formerly *Minimal-ish*), hosted by Desirae Endres
- *Feel Good Effect*, hosted by Robyn Conley Downs
- *Find the Magic*, hosted by Felica Allen, Taralyn Griffin, and Katelin Gabriel
- *Respectful Parenting: Janet Lansbury Unruffled*, hosted by Janet Lansbury

YOUTUBE

- Sarah Therese: On Sarah's channel, she dedicates a lot of her time and energy to minimalism. For someone that's a more visual learner (or is looking to combat their mindless television habit), this is a great place for info!

ACKNOWLEDGEMENTS

I cannot believe this project has come to fruition. I had always dreamed of writing a book but never thought that dream would come true. In a non-cliché way, I'd like to foremost thank God for creating within me that aptitude for creativity. The human mind is such a glorious miracle that I'll forever be in awe of.

Thank you to my husband for the many park outings he endured with our three children as I spent time writing and organizing my thoughts. More seriously, thank you for always being my biggest supporter, sacrificing your own leisure to make my dreams happen.

Thank you to my children for giving me the content to fill this book. Through all the ups and downs of parenting, I'm so grateful and blessed to be your mom.

Natasha Vera: I'll never forget receiving that initial email from you asking if I'd ever considered writing a book. I thank you for your guidance and personal investment in me throughout this entire process.

To Mango Publishing, for allowing me this opportunity. Thank you, thank you!

To mom and dad for listening to my writing throughout adolescence and early adulthood. You've always been my biggest supporters and I'll always be grateful for your unconditional love.

To my trio of 'Tier One' friends (ha!): Michelle, Kelsey and Grace. Thank you for extending a listening ear whenever I needed advice or wisdom throughout my writing process. You three keep me sane.

And a huge thank-you to the members of the Minimalist Moms community. Your support and encouragement throughout the release of the podcast and now the book have been amazing to see. Without you all tuning in week after week, this book never have been born.

BIBLIOGRAPHY

Adcock, Steve. "Does the American Dream Require a Big
    American Home?" *Get Rich Slowly* (blog), May 21, 2018.
    https://www.getrichslowly.org/american-home/.

Arnold, Jeanne E., Anthony P. Graesch, Enzo Ragazzini, and
    Elinor Ochs. *Life At Home in the Twenty-First Century:
    32 Families Open Their Doors*. Los Angeles: The Cotsen
    Institute of Archaeology Press, 2012.

Division of Sleep Medicine at Harvard Medical School.
    "Benefits of Sleep." Healthy Sleep. http://healthysleep.med.
    harvard.edu/healthy/matters/benefits-of-sleep.

Kondo, Marie. *The Life-Changing Magic of Tidying Up: The
    Japanese Art of Decluttering and Organizing*. Berkeley, CA:
    Ten Speed Press, 2014.

Lexico, "need (v.)," https://www.lexico.com/en/
    definition/need.

Lexico, "priority," https://www.lexico.com/definition/priority.

Martin, Karen. *The Outstanding Organization: Generate
    Business Results By Eliminating Chaos and Building the
    Foundation for Everyday Excellence*. New York: McGraw-Hill
    Education, 2012.

Merriam-Webster, "favorite, " https://www.merriam-webster.
   com/dictionary/favorite.

Merriam-Webster, "quantity," https://www.merriam-webster.
   com/dictionary/quantity.

Merriam-Webster, "sustainable," https://www.merriam-webster.
   com/dictionary/sustainable.

Muller, Wayne. *Sabbath: Finding Rest, Renewal, and Delight in
   Our Busy Lives*. New York: Bantam Books, 1999.

Newport, Cal. *Digital Minimalism: Choosing a Focused Life in a
   Noisy World.* New York: Portfolio, 2019.

Payne, Kim John, and Lisa M. Ross. *Simplicity Parenting*. New
   York: Ballantine Books, 2009.

Rathje, William L. "A Manifesto for Modern Material-Culture
   Studies." In *Modern Material Culture: The Archaeology of Us*,
   edited by Richard A. Gould and Michael B. Schiffer, 51-56.
   New York: Academic Press, 1981.

Rubin, Gretchen. "Need a Simple and Effective Way to Get
   Your Life Under Control? Try the 'One-Minute Rule.'"
   Gretchen Rubin (blog), December 15, 2006. https://
   gretchenrubin.com/2006/12/need_a_simple_a.

Seferian, Stephanie. "051: How to Handle Holiday Clutter with Joshua Becker." December 17, 2018. In *Sustainable Minimalists*, podcast, MP3 audio. http://mamaminimalist. com/051/?utm_source=rss&utm_medium=rss&utm_ campaign=051.

Sichelman, Lew. "Beware of Household Overflow: All That Stuff Causes Stress and Waste." *Hartford Courant*, October 31, 2018. https://www.courant.com/business/hc-hre-household-overflow-20181104-story.html.

Suni, Eric. "How Much Sleep Do We Really Need?" SleepFoundation.org, July 31, 2020. https://www. sleepfoundation.org/articles/how-much-sleep-do-we-really-need.

ABOUT THE AUTHOR

Diane Boden is the voice behind the top-rated podcast, *Minimalist Moms*, where she spreads her ideas and interviews others on living a life in pursuit of less. Her goal is simply this: think more and do with less. Diane has been a guest on *Find the Magic*, *Millennial Minimalists*, *With Intention Podcast*, and many others. She was featured in *(614) Magazine* in August 2019. She lives in Columbus, Ohio, with her husband and three children. You can follow her at @diane_boden on Instagram. You can also follow the podcast at @minimalistmomspodcast on Instagram or "like" the Minimalist Moms page on Facebook to get weekly motivation and encouragement. This is her first book.

Mango Publishing, established in 2014, publishes an eclectic list of books by diverse authors—both new and established voices—on topics ranging from business, personal growth, women's empowerment, LGBTQ studies, health, and spirituality to history, popular culture, time management, decluttering, lifestyle, mental wellness, aging, and sustainable living. We were recently named 2019 and 2020's #1 fastest growing independent publisher by *Publishers Weekly*. Our success is driven by our main goal, which is to publish high quality books that will entertain readers as well as make a positive difference in their lives.

Our readers are our most important resource; we value your input, suggestions, and ideas. We'd love to hear from you—after all, we are publishing books for you!

Please stay in touch with us and follow us at:

Facebook: Mango Publishing
Twitter: @MangoPublishing
Instagram: @MangoPublishing
LinkedIn: Mango Publishing
Pinterest: Mango Publishing
Newsletter: mangopublishinggroup.com/newsletter

Join us on Mango's journey to reinvent publishing, one book at a time.